ADRIS

D1231937

GEORGE MACDONALD

A Bibliographical Study

WITHDRAWN
C - / 13 / 2022
SAINT LOUIS UNIVERSITY

This edition, signed by the author, is limited
to 500 copies for sale

GEORGE MACDONALD

A Bibliographical Study

RAPHAEL B. SHABERMAN

St. Paul's Bibliographies
Winchester · Hampshire

Omnigraphics
Penobscot Building · Detroit

1990

PR
4968
.S52
1990

First published in Great Britain in 1990 by
St. Paul's Bibliographies, 1 Step Terrace,
Winchester, Hampshire
and in the United States by
Omnigraphics, Penobscot Building, Detroit

© 1990 Raphael B. Shaberman

British Library Cataloguing in Publication Data
Shaberman, R. B.
George MacDonald: A Bibliographical Study.
(19th Century Authors, 9).
1. Children's stories in English. MacDonald,
George, 1824–1905 – Bibliographies
I. Title   II. Series
016.8238

ISBN 0–906795–84–2

Library of Congress Catalog Card Number 89–50389

Typeset by Nene Phototypesetters Ltd, Northampton
∞ Printed on long-life paper by
Henry Ling Ltd, The Dorset Press, Dorchester
and bound by Green Street Bindery, Oxford

CONTENTS

LIST OF ILLUSTRATIONS

PREFACE AND ACKNOWLEDGEMENTS

The growing interest in the writings of George MacDonald (1824–1905) has prompted the production of this bibliographical study. It is the first to appear with any claim to comprehensiveness since J. M. Bulloch's *Centennial Bibliography of George MacDonald* was published in 1925, in an edition of only 50 copies. Bulloch's arrangement was alphabetical; in the present work it is chronological, thus making it easier to follow the progress of MacDonald's creative development.

This study covers the period up to 1974, the 150th anniversary of the author's birth. Items in the 'Supplementary Material' include unpublished letters by George MacDonald and Alexander Strahan, one of MacDonald's principal publishers: these appear by courtesy of the George MacDonald Society. The articles which comprise Appendices A and B are here published in book form for the first time, having previously appeared in slightly altered form in the journal of the George MacDonald Society. In addition the articles 'An Invalid's Winter in Algeria' and 'A Journey Rejourneyed' are here documented and reprinted for the first time. 'George MacDonald and Lewis Carroll' had its origin in a talk given to the Lewis Carroll Society of London in 1976.

Grateful acknowledgements are due to Robert Cross; Denis Crutch; R. A. Gilbert; Ian Kenyur-Hodgkins; John Kinnane; Mary Nance Jordan; Freda Levson; Christopher MacDonald; the Rev. John Pridmore; and the Rev. Phil Streeter, for their help and encouragement, in some cases extending over many years. The facilities afforded by the British Library, London, are also greatly appreciated.

INTRODUCTION

The writings of George MacDonald encompass, with almost mathematical precision, the second half of the nineteenth century. Like most other Victorian writers, the majority of his works first saw the light of day in the magazines which proliferated during that period. There followed publication in three-volume form, with the one-volume edition appearing shortly after. That there should be revisions as between one edition and another was not in itself unusual. However, MacDonald gave us virtually no clues as to their extent or time of first publication. For example, 'The Portent' appeared in book form in 1864, with a note stating that the book 'is a portion reprinted from the "Cornhill Magazine" and completed'. We are not told when the story first appeared, and by how much it was extended. In fact it was published anonymously in 1860, and was increased in length by about half in 1864. Furthermore, the emphasis of the story was changed. The first version, which some would consider better than the second, has never been reprinted.

Again, the second edition of *Adela Cathcart* differs so much from the first (1864) that it is really a different book, though with the same title and framework. (It should be noted that the term 'new edition' was often used in Victorian times for a simple reprint from the same typesetting.) To give a further example, in the collection of translations which he called *Exotics* (1876), MacDonald wrote that the preface and the Luther translations 'was first uttered some years ago in a periodical'. But how does one begin to search for 'a periodical' that appeared 'some years ago'? It so happened that, quite by chance, the present writer discovered them in a book fair, in a bound volume for 1866 of *The Sunday Magazine*. Such a discovery is gratifying when it occurs, but it brings to MacDonaldian bibliography a substantial element of Nesbitian treasure-seeking.

Another problem is the range of subject matter, which is much wider in MacDonald than in other authors. In Part II, all the titles are presented chronologically: the purpose of Part I is to make clear this range by presenting the titles under subject headings, and is simplified for easy reference. For example, it will be seen at once that the novels comprise by far the greater part of his output. The headings in Part I would appear to suggest themselves naturally, but their selection was inevitably subjective to some extent.

The core of the present study is Part II. It will be seen, from a perusal of Part I, that any attempt to subdivide would result in excessive fragmentation, and make it difficult to perceive the pattern of Mac-Donald's development. For it is the guiding principle of this work that it presents, or attempts to present, the pattern of MacDonald's creative evolution. For this reason, Part II is entirely chronological, with as many 'first publications' (i.e. in magazines) as possible given separately in the year of publication. Again, it would, in one sense, be simpler to place the Novalis translations of 1851 and those of 1873 under 'Exotics', 1876. Yet so important an influence was Novalis on MacDonald that the 1851 translations must stand at the beginning of this bibliography where they rightly belong, chronologically as well as influentially. MacDonald did not translate to earn money – for him, it was a true labour of love. Almost the last work he had published was *Rampolli* (1897), an extension of *Exotics*. To say that MacDonald began and ended his writing career with Novalis is almost literally true. It must be added that the other German Romantic writers also exercised a considerable influence on MacDonald.

Because this bibliography proceeds chronologically, it will readily be seen that MacDonald made a slow and late beginning. Up to the time of *David Elginbrod*, 1863, he had had only three books published – *Within and Without* (1855), *Poems* (1857), and *Phantastes* (1858). He was then 39. But the next two decades saw a remarkable outpouring of works of all kinds – and this from an author who was plagued with bronchial ailments for most of his life, and had a wife and 13 children to support! Thereafter he slowed down, yet produced, quite unexpectedly, that extraordinary fantasy *Lilith* in 1895. His last years were spent in a state of complete withdrawal, in a condition that was never positively diagnosed.

One non-existent item has been included – the unpublished novel *Seekers and Finders* (*c.*1860), which the author's son Greville destroyed. Can we be sure that no copy of this work has survived? The fact remains that George MacDonald wrote it, and who can tell what will be washed up by the seas of Time on some remote shore? Greville also destroyed the 1894 edition of *Phantastes* because he and his mother disliked the illustrations. He was certainly not successful in suppressing this edition, because many copies have survived. As for George MacDonald, he seemed as indifferent to this matter as to helping future bibliographers.

Thus we pass – or should we say ascend – from the problematical to the mysterious. Why did not Arthur Hughes illustrate *The Princess and Curdie* when he had illustrated the first *Princess* book? Why did *Curdie* have to wait five years from the magazine publication (1877) to its appearance in book form in 1882? What is much more remarkable is the advertisement that appeared in an undated edition of *Paul Faber, Surgeon* published by Strahan, as follows:

'*The Princess and Curdie: A New Fairy Romance*
Crown 8vo, cloth, gilt edges, 5s.'

The name of Arthur Hughes as illustrator is not given. This advertisement, whenever it appeared, reveals that preparations for its issue were well advanced. Yet the book was not published by Strahan, but by Chatto and Windus. We may well ask, what went wrong? The loss is certainly ours, for in Arthur Hughes, MacDonald found his ideal illustrator, the two standing in the same relationship to each other as John Tenniel and Lewis Carroll – indeed the latter had seen some Hughes illustrations to *The Light Princess* as early as 1862, five years before the first edition of *Dealings with Fairies*. However, prompted by MacDonald's son Greville, Hughes in his late years illustrated the 1905 edition of *Phantastes*, as well as some of the fairy tales of Greville MacDonald, themselves strongly influenced by those of his illustrious father.

CHRONOLOGY OF
GEORGE MACDONALD'S LIFE

1824   Born December 10 at Huntly, Aberdeenshire.

1832   Death of his mother.

1839   His father remarries.

1840   Attends King's College, Aberdeen, after winning a bursary. Studies Maths, Languages, Chemistry.

1845   Takes MA degree: moves to London.

1848   Attends Highbury (Congregational) College. Engagement to Louisa Powell.

1850   Becomes Congregationalist Minister at Arundel, Sussex. November: illness necessitates convalescence. He stays at Niton and Newport, Isle of Wight. Begins writing *Within and Without*.

1851   Marries Louisa Powell, March 8. *Twelve of the Spiritual Songs of Novalis* printed privately and distributed as a Christmas gift to his friends.

1852   His first child, Lilia, born January 4.

1853   Because of his allegedly unorthodox views, he is forced to resign as minister at Arundel. Moves to Manchester.

1855   *Within and Without*, his first published book, which attracts the attention of Lady Byron.

1856   His first son and future biographer, Greville, born January 20. November: leaves for Algiers, a trip made possible by the generosity of Lady Byron.

1857   April: Returns from Algiers. June: first meeting with Lady Byron, *Poems* published. October: moves to Hastings.

1858   His first meeting with C. L. Dodgson ('Lewis Carroll'). Publication of his first novel, *Phantastes*. August: death of his father. November 6: birth of Winifred.

1859   Moves to London. Lectures in Edinburgh, Manchester and London, as Professor of English at Bedford College.

1860   Death of Lady Byron. Anonymous publication of *The Portent*.

1862   July 9. Shows Lewis Carroll the MS of *The Light Princess* with illustrations by Arthur Hughes, while walking near Regent's Park.

1863 The MacDonald family read the MS of *Alice's Adventures Under Ground* (published in 1865 as *Alice's Adventures in Wonderland*). They urge Lewis Carroll to publish it. Publication of *David Elginbrod*, MacDonald's first '3-decker'. First meeting with John Ruskin.

1864 *Adela Cathcart* (3 vols); *The Portent*.

1865 *Alec Forbes of Howglen* (3 vols). Takes a summer holiday in Switzerland.

1867 Moves to 'The Retreat', Hammersmith (later the home of William Morris). *Dealings with the Fairies*; *Unspoken Sermons* (first series); *Annals of a Quiet Neighbourhood* (3 vols). *The Disciple*. MacDonald now in his most productive period.

1868 *Guild Court* (3 vols); *Robert Falconer* (3 vols); *The Seaboard Parish* (3 vols); *England's Antiphon*. Awarded honorary doctorate by Aberdeen University.

1869 Edits *Good Words for the Young*, in which all his 'long' fairy stories first appear.

1870 *The Miracles of Our Lord*.

1871 *At the Back of the North Wind*; *Ranald Bannerman's Boyhood*; *Works of Fancy and Imagination* (10 vols – the first collected edition).

1872 Successful lecture tour of the USA. *The Princess and the Goblin*; *Wilfred Cumbermede* (3 vols); *The Vicar's Daughter* (3 vols).

1873 Resigns editorship of *Good Words for the Young*. *Gutta Percha Willie*.

1875 Moves to Boscombe, Hampshire. *The Wise Woman*; *Malcolm* (3 vols).

1876 *Exotics*; *St. George and St. Michael* (3 vols); *Thomas Wingfold, Curate* (3 vols).

1877 The MacDonald family give their first performance of Bunyan's *The Pilgrim's Progress*. *The Marquis of Lossie* (3 vols). MacDonald awarded Civil List Pension. First visit to Italy (Liguria).

1878 Death of his daughter Mary, at Nervi.

1879 *Paul Faber, Surgeon* (3 vols); *Sir Gibbie* (3 vols). Death of his son Maurice, at Porto Fino.

1880 *Diary of an Old Soul*. The MacDonalds move to Bordighera, Liguria.

1881 *Mary Marston* (3 vols); *Warlock o' Glen Warlock*.

1882 *Weighed and Wanting* (3 vols); *Orts*; *The Gifts of the Child Christ* (2 vols).

1883 *The Princess and Curdie*; *Donal Grant* (3 vols); *A Threefold Cord*.

1884 Death of his daughter Grace.

1885 *Unspoken Sermons* (2nd series); *The Tragedie of Hamlet*.

1886 *What's Mine's Mine* (3 vols).

1887 *Home Again*.

1888 *The Elect Lady*.

1889   *Unspoken Sermons* (3rd series).
1891   *The Flight of the Shadow*; *A Rough Shaking*; *There and Back*, the last 3-volume novel. Death of his daughter Lilia.
1892   *The Hope of the Gospel.*
1893   *The Poetical Works* (2 vols); *Heather and Snow* (2 vols).
1895   *Lilith.*
1897   *Salted with Fire*; *Rampolli.*
1898   *Far above Rubies*, MacDonald's last published work. After a period of ill-health, he lapses into a condition of withdrawal for which no precise diagnosis has been given.
1902   January 13. His wife Louisa dies at Bordighera.
1905   September 18. George MacDonald dies at Ashstead, Surrey. His ashes are buried at Bordighera next to those of his wife.

Note: The MacDonald family as a whole were afflicted by the bronchial ailments that were all too common in Victorian times. The moves of the MacDonalds, to Algiers, Boscombe and Italy, for example, were undertaken for health reasons. Even so, they were not spared the deaths of four of their eleven children. MacDonald named his house in Bordighera 'Casa Corragio' ('The House of Courage'), and an anagram of his name, 'Corage, God mend al' was incorporated into the design of his bookplate. His achievements as an author must be seen, among other things, as the fruits of his constant struggle against ill-health.

PART I

A CLASSIFIED HANDLIST OF FIRST EDITIONS

The first editions of George MacDonald's books are here classified according to subject, the arrangement being chronological in each group. Unless otherwise stated, works are in one volume and published in London. The subjects are: (i) Poetry, (ii) Novels, (iii) Books for Children, (iv) Sermons, (v) Translations by George MacDonald, (vi) Essays and Criticism, (vii) Collected Works, (viii) Miscellaneous. The entry number follows in parentheses.

(i) POETRY

1855   *Within and Without* (6)
1857   *Poems* (7)
1867   *The Disciple and Other Poems* (34)
1880   *A Book of Strife in the form of The Diary of an Old Soul* (66)
[1883] *A Threefold Cord: Poems by Three Friends* (75)
[1886] *An Old Story* (81)

(ii) NOVELS

1858   *Phantastes: A Faerie Romance for Men and Women* (8)
1863   *David Elginbrod* (3 vols) (14)
1864   *Adela Cathcart* (3 vols) (17)
1864   *The Portent: a story of the inner vision of the Highlanders, commonly called The Second Sight* (18)
1865   *Alec Forbes of Howglen* (3 vols) (20)
1867   *Annals of a Quiet Neighbourhood* (3 vols) (28)
1868   *Guild Court* (3 vols) (35)
1868   *Robet Falconer* (3 vols) (36)
1868   *The Seaboard Parish* (3 vols) (38)
1872   *Wilfred Cumbermede* (3 vols) (47)

1

1872 *The Vicar's Daughter: An Autobiographical Story* (3 vols) (49)
1875 *Malcolm* (3 vols) (52)
1876 *St. George and St. Michael* (3 vols) (55)
1876 *Thomas Wingfold, Curate* (3 vols) (59)
1877 *The Marquis of Lossie* (3 vols) (61)
1879 *Paul Faber, Surgeon* (3 vols) (63)
1879 *Sir Gibbie* (3 vols) (64)
1881 *Mary Marston* (3 vols) (67)
1881 *Warlock O'Glen Warlock: A Homely Romance.* Boston, USA (68A)
1882 *Castle Warlock: A Homely Romance.* First UK edition of the above (3 vols) (69)
1882 *Weighed and Wanting* (3 vols) (73)
1883 *Donal Grant* (3 vols) (76)
1886 *What's Mine's Mine* (3 vols) (80)
1887 *Home Again* (82)
1888 *The Elect Lady* (84)
1891 *There and Back* (3 vols) (88)
1891 *The Flight of the Shadow* (90)
1893 *Heather and Snow: A Novel* (2 vols) (93)
1895 *Lilith: A Romance* (97)
1897 *Salted with Fire* (100)
1899 *Far Above Rubies.* New York, USA. Not published in book form in UK (101)

(iii) BOOKS FOR CHILDREN

1867 *Dealings with the Fairies* (31)
1871 *At the Back of the North Wind* (43)
1871 *Ranald Bannerman's Boyhood* (46)
1872 *The Princess and the Goblin* (48)
1873 *Gutta Percha Willie, the Working Genius* (51)
1875 *The Wise Woman: A Parable* (54)
1883 *The Princess and Curdie* (74)
1891 *A Rough Shaking* (89)

(iv) SERMONS

1867 *Unspoken Sermons* (29)
1870 *The Miracles of Our Lord* (41)
1885 *Unspoken Sermons, Second Series* (79)
1889 *Unspoken Sermons, Third Series* (85)
1892 *The Hope of the Gospel* (92)

(v) TRANSLATIONS BY GEORGE MACDONALD

1851 *Twelve of the Spiritual Songs of Novalis* (Issued privately on Christmas Day, 1851) (1)

1876   *Exotics: A Translation of the Spiritual Songs of Novalis, the Hymn Book of Luther, and other poems from the German and Italian* (60)

1897   *Rampolli: Growths from a Long-planted Root, being Translations, New and Old, chiefly from the German, along with A Year's Diary of An Old Soul* (99)

(vi) ESSAYS AND CRITICISM

[1868] *England's Antiphon* (39)

1882   *Orts* (72)

1885   *The Tragedie of Hamlet, Prince of Denmarke; a Study with the text of the Folio of 1623* (78)

1893   *A Dish of Orts, chiefly papers on the Imagination, and on Shakspere.* (An enlarged version of *Orts*, 1882) (94)

(vii) COLLECTED WORKS

1871   *Works of Fancy and Imagination* (10 vols) (44)

1893   *The Poetical Works* (2 vols) (95)

(viii) MISCELLANEOUS

1882   *The Gifts of the Child Christ, and Other Tales* (2 vols) (71)

1892   *A Cabinet of Gems* (Extracts from Sir Philip Sidney, edited by George MacDonald) (91)

PART II

WORKS BY GEORGE MACDONALD

References:

Life = *George MacDonald and his Wife*, by Greville MacDonald: George Allen & Unwin, 1924.

Bulloch = *A Centennial Bibliography of George MacDonald*, by John Malcolm Bulloch: The University Press, Aberdeen, 1925.

Wolff = *The Golden Key: A Study of the Fiction of George MacDonald*, by Robert Lee Wolff: Yale University Press, New Haven, 1961.

Place of publication is London, unless otherwise stated.

1851

1. TWELVE OF THE SPIRITUAL SONGS OF NOVALIS. Christmas Day, 1851.

Translated from the German and issued privately from Arundel as a Christmas present to his friends, this was George MacDonald's first book. Only three copies have hitherto been recorded:

(i) Greville MacDonald's copy, described by Bulloch, p.47. 'Some of the pages have coloured decorations of flowers by George MacDonald's wife.'

(ii) The Brander Library (Huntly) copy, which has marginal corrections in ink to the fifth verse of the eighth song (recorded by Muriel Hutton in 'The George MacDonald Collection, Brander Library, Huntly', 'The Book Collector', Spring, 1968).

(iii) The Houghton Library (Harvard) copy, which lacks the title leaf.

The following description is by Bulloch:

9×5¾ ins: ppi–iv+(3)–27+(1). Imprint on last page: Arundel: printed by Mitchell & Son, High Street.

The preface, dated Arundel, December 25, 1851, states that the author had 'the distant hope of one day offering the works of Novalis in an English garb to English readers'. This was not fulfilled, but MacDonald produced extended versions of this work in 1873 (privately printed), 1876 *(Exotics)* and 1897 *(Rampolli)*, indicating the influence of Novalis from an early stage in his development until virtually the end of his creative life. (See Bulloch, pp.47, 48 and Wolff, pp.10, 11, 388, 389.)

1853

2. BROWNING'S 'CHRISTMAS EVE'. Signed 'G.M.D.' *Monthly Christian Spectator*, May, 1853; iii, 261–73.

In a letter to his father dated May 20, 1853, he wrote that the editor had asked him to delete 'the most important portion' *(Life,* p.185).

1873 Reprinted in *Day of Rest*; Jan. 18 and 25, i, 34–6, 55–6.

1882 Reprinted in *Orts*.

1883 Reprinted in *A Dish of Orts*.

[1853]

3. REVIEW OF 'ESSAYS ON SOME OF THE FORMS OF LITERATURE', BY THOMAS TOKE LYNCH, 1853.

This was reprinted in *Orts*, 1882, and *A Dish of Orts*, 1893, without giving the name or date of the publication in which it originally appeared.

1854

4. THE BROKEN SWORDS. Signed 'XXX'. *Monthly Christian Spectator*, October, 1854; iv, 633–40.

This, his first published story, was reprinted in the first edition of *Adela Cathcart*, 1864 (vol.ii, pp.208–60), but was omitted from the 1882 edition.

1871 Reprinted in *Works of Fancy and Imagination*.

[1909] Reprinted in *The Portent and other stories* (Fisher Unwin).

1973 Reprinted in the Eerdmans/Mowbray collection – see under *The Gifts of the Child Christ*, 1882.

1855

5. [Contributions to] HYMNS AND SACRED SONGS, FOR SUNDAY SCHOOLS AND SOCIAL WORSHIP. Fletcher & Tubbs, Manchester, and Hamilton Adams, London. 1855.

32mo; pp.256. With a preface, signed 'B', dated Manchester, May 1, 1855, and an index which identifies George MacDonald as 'G. B. MacDonald'. 'B' was the Rev. George Burden Bubier, who edited this collection of 318 hymns in association with George MacDonald and the latter's brother Charles. George MacDonald contributed 10 hymns, including one from Novalis ('If I Him but have', reprinted in *Exotics*, 1876, and *Rampolli*, 1897). Some data concerning Bubier are given in Joseph Johnson's *George MacDonald*, 1906, pp.41–4.

Reprinted 1856, 1858, 1866.

1855

6. WITHIN AND WITHOUT: A Dramatic Poem. By George Mac Donald. Longman, Brown, Green and Longmans, [May 18] 1855.

8vo: pp.[iv], 184+28 adv., dated March, 1855. Brown cloth, gilt spine, plain edges, price 7*s*. 6*d*. Motto on title-page (p.[i]):

> 'What life it is, and how that all these lives do gather –
> With outward maker's force, or like an inward father.'
> Sir Philip Sidney's *Arcadia*

This drama in blank verse was George MacDonald's first published book, dedicated 'To L.P.M.D.' (his wife, Louisa Powell MacDonald), in a sonnet dated May, 1855 (p.[iii]), which relates the circumstances of the composition of the poem:

> Receive thine own; for I and it are thine.
> Thou know'st its story; how for forty days –
> Weary with sickness and with social haze,
> (After thy hands and lips with love divine
> Had somewhat soothed me, made the glory shine,
> Though with a watery lustre,) more delays
> Of blessedness forbid – I took my ways

J. B. Metcalfe Esq. from his obliged friend, George Mac Donald.

WITHIN AND WITHOUT:

A

DRAMATIC POEM.

BY GEORGE MAC DONALD.

"What life it is, and how that all these lives do gather—
With outward maker's force, or like an inward father."
SIR PHILIP SIDNEY'S *Arcadia*.

LONDON:
LONGMAN, BROWN, GREEN, AND LONGMANS.
1855.

1. Title page of *Within and Without* (1855), GMD's first published book
with an inscription by the author.

Into a solitude, Invention's mine;
There thought and wrote, afar, and yet with thee.
Those days gone past, I came, and brought a book;
My child, developed since in limb and look.
It came in shining vapours from the sea,
And in thy stead sung low sweet songs to me,
When the red life-blood labour would not brook.

The 'forty days' refer to his stay at Newport and Niton, on the Isle of Wight, from Dec. 1850 to Jan. 1851: it was there that he wrote the poem. Newport is in the centre of the island, but Niton is near the sea, hence the significance of 'the shining vapours from the sea'. The 'sickness' refers to the bronchial ailments that afflicted him for most of his life. He maintained constant contact with his wife by letter: the following is from one dated Niton, Dec. 27, 1850:

'. . . I shall write a little of my poem this evening.
I fear it will disappoint me as usual . . .' (*Life*, p.149)

He did not complete revising until early in 1854 (ibid., p.218). The title comes from Blake's *Jerusalem*:

'God is within and without, even in the depths of Hell.'

MacDonald was a lifelong admirer of Blake; his bookplate embodied one of his designs. The poem in Part IV, Sc.i, beginning 'Love me, beloved', was a wedding present to his wife – it was 'with some real touch of heart-break' that she consented to its publication (ibid., p.224). A fine hand-written copy of the book was made by MacDonald and presented to his wife: her father read it 'with tears streaming down his stern old face' (ibid., p.221). On March 17, 1854, he informed his father that the book was in the hands of an Edinburgh publisher. It was refused, then Macmillan turned it down, but on February 7, 1855, Longmans signed an agreement to publish, and the book appeared on May 18.

It was, on the whole, well received.

'. . . the reviews were so enthusiastic that it was determined to advertise it largely with extracts from the Press; though, seeing that some inevitably were foolish, some cynical, and some even spiteful, the author thought the unfavourable ones should be given the same publicity as the enthusiastic ones – an opinion that did not tally with the publishers' ' (*Life*, p.223).

The Scotsman wrote:

'This strange and original drama is full of the most exquisite poetry sustained at the pitch of sublimity with immense yet apparently effortless power . . . A very remarkable production of intellect and heart united as perhaps they seldom have been before . . .'

But the *Athenaeum* (July 7, 1855: p.783) found 'the whole inexpressibly painful . . . and there is a want of comprehension'. The longest review was in the *Monthly Christian Spectator* (August, 1855: v, 503–8), to which MacDonald was a contributor.

MacDonald wrote an analysis of the poem for Longman's quarterly, *Notes on Books*, beginning:

'This poem is an attempt to represent the history of a man who, *apparently* disappointed in all his secondary aims and hopes, attains, partly through means of these disappointments, to the freedom of faith; and finds that in gaining this he has gained everything, in a higher form, too, than he had ever anticipated . . .'

(This analysis is given, in an abridged form, in the *Life*, pp.224–5. Joseph Johnson devotes 24 pages to this book in his *George MacDonald*, 1906.)

The publication of *Within and Without* led to new and important friendships. Lady Byron wrote to MacDonald soon after the book appeared, for around August, 1855, he wrote to his father 'of the interest Lady Byron, the widow of the poet, has taken in it. It seems to have taken a powerful hold on her' (*Life*, p.249).

1857   Second edition. Published by Longman, Brown, Green, Longmans, and Roberts. 8vo; pp.iv, 193, (1), +26 adv, dated March, 1856. Brown cloth.

1871   Reprinted in *Works of Fancy and Imagination*, 1871.

1872   First American publication. Published by Scribner, Armstrong, New York: 12mo, pp.219. From the review in *Scribners' Monthly*, May, 1872, Bulloch deduced that Scribners advertised it as 'a thrilling story in verse'.

1893   Reprinted in *The Poetical Works*, vol.i (q.v.).

1857

7. POEMS. By George MacDonald. Longman, Brown, Green, Longmans and Roberts, [August] 1857.

8vo: pp.viii, 395, (1). Motto: 6 lines from the Inferno, Cant. 1.

Dedicated to his father, in two sonnets, dated Algiers, April, 1857, and signed 'G.M.D.jr.'. The trip to Algiers, undertaken for health reasons, was assisted and probably proposed by Lady Byron, who provided travelling expenses (*Life*, p.266). He first met Lady Byron, after his return from Algiers, in June, 1857.

This collection comprises 92 poems (excluding the two dedicatory sonnets). It begins with the long autobiographical poem 'A Hidden Life' (pp.3–52), and includes 'A Book of Dreams' (pp.74–110); a group of 18 sonnets 'About Jesus' (pp.287–304); 'Death and Birth: A Symbol', with marginal annotations (pp.305–18); a group of eight 'Early Poems', undated (pp.321–45); and 'The Gospel Women', a group of 16 poems (pp.349–95).

1864   Published as *A Hidden Life and other poems* by Longmans.

1871   Reprinted in *Works of Fancy and Imagination* (q.v.).

1872   Published as *A Hidden Life and other poems* by Scribner, Armstrong, New York.

1893   Reprinted in *The Poetical Works* (q.v.).

1858

8.   PHANTASTES: A Faerie Romance for Men and Women. By George MacDonald. Smith, Elder & Co., [Oct.] 1858.

8vo: pp.iv, 323, (1), (16 adv. dated Sept. 1858). Olive-green cloth; gilt spine *(Phantastes: A Faerie Romance)*; covers blind-stamped; plain edges; price 10s. 6d.

Mottoes:
p.i (half-title: *Phantastes: A Faerie Romance*):
         'Phantastes from "their fount" all shapes deriving.
         In new habiliments can quickly dight.
         Fletcher's Purple Island.' [1633].
p.ii: two passages from Novalis, in German.
p.iii (title page):
         'In good sooth, my masters, this is no door.
         Yet is it a little window, that looketh upon a great world.'
Each chapter is prefaced by at least one motto. The story is interspersed with poems.

This was MacDonald's first story to be published in book form: it took him two months to write, and he sold it for £50, including the copyright. *The Athenaeum* described it as 'a confusedly furnished, second-hand symbol shop'. It forms a natural companion to *Lilith*, published nearly forty years later, both works revealing to a marked degree the influence of 'Heinrich von Ofterdingen' of Novalis.

(*c.*1870)   First American publication. Published by Loring; Boston (USA): 12mo, pp.286.

1871   Reprinted in *Works of Fancy and Imagination* (q.v.).

1885   Published as no.1922 of *Munro's Seaside Library*, New York, and as no.236 of the pocket edition of that series.

1894 Published by Chatto & Windus as *Phantastes: A Faerie Romance.* 8vo, pp.vii, 280, with 25 illustrations by John Bell. This edition was suppressed by Greville MacDonald because, as he claimed, the illustrations were unauthorised, and so unsuitable 'that all lovers of the book must have experienced some real grief in turning its pages. With the copyright I secured also the whole of that edition and turned it into pulp'. (Preface to the 1905 edition of *Phantastes*, which replaced the edition of 1894, and was illustrated by Arthur Hughes at the request of Greville MacDonald.)

There is some mystery concerning this suppression. Bulloch states that Bell's illustrations 'caused [George] MacDonald accute distress' (p.34). Yet the *Life* makes no mention of this, nor of the 1894 edition. The second edition of *Lilith* (1896), also published by Chatto & Windus, included an advertisement for the 1894 *Phantastes*, quoting the *Saturday Review*:

'... a pretty edition ... which Mr. Bell has illustrated with considerable sympathy and grace.'

Bulloch went on to say that he knew of only one copy. However, this edition is by no means scarce; we have seen one copy with ads dated 1901. Apparently George MacDonald did not know of the 1894 illustrations, or if he did he was not unduly concerned. Greville did not reveal the date of his purchase of the 1894 edition, nor did he state that the purchase was authorised by his father. Further details were published by Greville MacDonald in his *Reminiscences of a Specialist*, 1932, in which he quoted from an undated letter sent by his mother from Bordighera:

'... It made me groan – within me and aloud – that that wondrous "Phantastes" should have been so degraded by Sunday-at-homish, bad art. Have you seen its worse than pantomime scratchings of silly columbines and jumping jacks? That holy fairy book! I can't bear to think of it ... Oh! If only it had fallen into Arthur Hughes' hands! ...' (p.326).

Greville MacDonald continued:

'A few years later I re-purchased the copyright along with hundreds of "remainders", of which I destroyed the whole consignment. Then, following my mother's suggestion, I gave Arthur Hughes a free hand in illustrating it. That old friend was now almost past his best imaginative work; but his hand had not lost its cunning and the drawings had much of his early charm, while some were even strong' (ibid.).

1905 Published by Arthur C. Fifield: 8vo, pp.x, 320. With an introduction by Greville MacDonald (pp.vii, viii) dated September, 1905 and 33 new illustrations by Arthur Hughes. The original subtitle ('A Faerie Romance for Men and Women') is restored. Blue cloth, lettering on spine and front cover in gilt, top edge gilt. (Also issued in crushed morocco, but scarce thus.)

This superb edition fully justified Greville MacDonald's efforts in seeking the co-operation of Arthur Hughes, who was 73 when he completed these illustrations: the texture is lighter than his earlier work, but they are most evocative and perfectly match the mood of the story.

[1911]   Published by McKay, Philadelphia, with *The Portent*.

1915   Published as no.732 of Dent's 'Everyman Library', under the title *Phantastes, A Fäerie* [sic] *Romance by George MacDonald*. 8vo, pp.xii, 237. Introduction by Greville MacDonald. The publishers listed it as 'For Young People' (p.[i]): this was changed in 1923 (see *Life*, p.299). The first two titles in the bibliography should be reversed (p.x).

1923   As above, except that 'For Young People' has been replaced by 'Romance'.

1954   Published by Noonday Press, New York, together with *Lilith*. Edited by Anne Freemantle, introduced by W. H. Auden.

1962   Published by Gollancz with *Lilith* in one volume. Introduction by C. S. Lewis (pp.7–11), being a much abbreviated version of his preface to *George MacDonald; an Anthology* (1946). Reprinted 1971.

1964   As above, published by W. B. Eerdmans, Grand Rapids, USA.

1970   Published by Ballantine Books, London and New York, in their 'Adult Fantasy' series (paperback) as *Phantastes* (i.e. without subtitle). Introduction by Lin Carter. Cover-to-cover design in colour by Gervasio Gallardo. First US printing, 1970.

This edition omits all the poems, on the grounds that MacDonald 'had no ear for writing verse at all, and the intrusion of his saccharine rhymes injured, rather than enhanced, the strength and clearness of the book' (p.x). *Lilith* is a companion volume in this series.

1971   [December] First UK printing of above, price 40p.

1971   Reprint of Gollancz edition of 1962.

[? 1860]

9.   SEEKERS AND FINDERS: an unpublished novel.

Soon after the publication of *Phantastes* in 1858, MacDonald wrote a four-act play, *If I had a Father*. It was refused by George Murray Smith, of Smith, Elder & Co., the publishers of *Phantastes*, and was eventually published in *The Gifts of the Child Christ*, 1882. Around 1860, Mac-Donald turned it into a novel of some 120,000 words, with the title *Seekers and Finders*. This too was refused by Smith, Elder (their reader, W. Smith-Williams, wrote a criticism of the novel which came into the possession of Greville MacDonald). The novel was never published, and the manuscript was destroyed by Greville MacDonald around 1924. Ronald MacDonald (a brother of Greville) and Ernest Rhys (editor of *Everyman's Library*) also read the manuscript, and endorsed Greville's decision not to publish it (*Life*, p.319).

The only source of information concerning this novel is the *Life*, which gives the following resumé:

> 'With much suggestive utterance, epigrammatic diction and know-ledge of human nature in certain aspects, it is often theatrical in its presentation of characters, while its conversations are more like debates of some delegates in the audience-chamber of the writer's mind than real dialogue. Yet the book is wholly consistent with its writer's life-long convictions. Its central idea is not unlike that of *Within and Without*, though characters and narrative have nothing in common with that poem. Robert Falconer first appears here, though his own story is reserved for future telling. Like Julian, he stands for the prophet who primarily has vision of the truth always supreme to its concrete expression, while his antithesis, Aurelio, a young, im-aginative sculptor, finds in Beauty the manifestation of all Truth and so seeks to idealise Form without any further concept of what Truth means. Then, standing apart from each, is the idle young aristocrat with delicate and high-cultured feeling, who yet looks upon Beauty as if manifested for its own and his own sake. Naturally he is the bad influence of the story; and his father, a melodramatic yet imaginatively conceived Bluebeard, with a chamber of horrors – not for wives, but for men and women whom he has hated and loves chiefly for the sake of injuring – is horrible indeed. Yet it has many and great beauties. It reveals, too, the writer's intimacy with disreputable London. ... So my father's determination to leave this novel unpublished has been respected: and it is now destroyed' (*Life*, pp.319, 320).

The following quotations are all that survive of the text:

> 'The merely professional literary party was an abhorrence to him. He said it made him feel sick – he could not help it. He took more pleasure in smoking a pipe now and then with an old cobbler somewhere about

the Theobald's Road than in any evening with the most delightful literary society that London could furnish' (ibid., p.321).

Describing 'a certain gathering of fashionable intellect which Falconer feels constrained to attend' (ibid.):

'When he arrived he found the rooms quite up to the ordinary degree of crush and discomfort. Across the chaos of female cones and males obelisks, bowing and grinning, each with a veil of conventional fibre over the face, through which ever and anon a real thought and feeling peered and disappeared, he saw no one for some time that he knew ... amusing himself with ludicrous suggestions and wishing the ladies would come in their nightgowns instead of in go-carts and colanders ...' (ibid., pp. 321–2).

Spoken by Robert Falconer:

'Though one evil spirit may drive a woman out of Eden, all the devils in Hell cannot drive Heaven out of a woman!' (ibid., p.344).

And finally:

'The Soul of Man is the World turned outside in' (ibid., p.404).

1860

10.   THE PORTENT. A story of the supernatural, serialised anonymously in *The Cornhill Magazine*, May–July, 1860, in three parts: I – 'Its Legend' (May, vol.i, pp.617–30); II – 'The Omen Coming On' (June, vol.i, pp. 670–81); III – 'The Omen Fulfilled' (July, vol.ii, pp.74–83). The title of part II is a quotation from *Hamlet*. An illustration by W. J. Linton faces p.617 (vol.i).

This was the first of MacDonald's works to be serialised, the first to be illustrated, and also the first to be extensively revised on reappearing in book form in 1864 (q.v.).

1860

11.   An article on Shelley, signed 'G.M.D.', appeared in the *Encyclopaedia Britannica*, 8th edition, 1860, vol.xx, p.100; an enlarged version was included in *Orts*, 1882, and *A Dish of Orts*, 1893.

MacDonald wrote to Lady Byron on the subject of Shelley while preparing this article: her reply, dated August 6, 1859, is quoted in the *Life*, p.308.

1861

12.   MY UNCLE PETER. By George MacDonald.

This short Christmas story appeared in *The Queen*, Dec. 21, 1861, and was reprinted in *Adela Cathcart*, 1864 (q.v.). Two short poems by MacDonald also appeared in this number: 'Born on Christmas Eve', and 'Died on Christmas Eve', with one illustration for both poems by Arthur Hughes.

1862

13.   CROSS PURPOSES: A FAIRY TALE. By George MacDonald.

This, the first of MacDonald's fairy tales to be published, appeared in *Beeton's Christmas Annual*, 1862, pp.58–63. It was included in *Dealings with the Fairies*, 1867, with the addition of the Owl's song.

1863

14.   DAVID ELGINBROD. By George MacDonald, M.A. Hurst and Blackett, 1863.

8vo: 3 vols; vol.I – pp.viii, 325, (1); vol.II – pp.vii, 335, (1); vol.III – pp.vi, 398. Brick-red cloth. Dedicated to the memory of Lady Noel Byron (d.1860) 'with a love stronger than death'. Reviewed in the *Athenaeum*, January 17, 1863.

The germ of this novel was an epitaph related by Charles Manby Smith, a journalist, at a supper attended by MacDonald, who acknowledged this in a letter to Smith dated September 7, 1863 (*Life*, p.321). The epitaph appears in vol.I, ch.XIII:

> 'Here lie I, Martin Elginbrodde:
> Hae mercy o' my soul, Lord God;
> As I wad do, were I Lord God,
> And ye were Martin Elginbrodde.'

Bulloch believed that Smith probably got it from the *Essay towards the Theory of the Intelligible World*, written in 1700 by Gabriel John. Max Müller discussed the epitaph in the *Athenaeum* (May 14, 1887) finding Vedic analogies. Other versions, including French and German, were cited by correspondents to the *Sunday Times* (June 1, 8, 15, 22, July 13, 1924); the *Yorkshire Evening Post* (May 24, 1924); and *Notes and Queries* (July 5, 1924). Bulloch summarised these versions in the *Aberdeen University Review* (November, 1924).

The character of David Elginbrod was drawn from MacDonald's father; Funkelstein was based on the Polish mesmerist Zamoiski, whom Mac-Donald met in Hastings; and an Arundel archdeacon who gave him 'a good deal of trouble' was transformed into Appleditch, the grocer, in vol.III (Bulloch, p.16). C. L. Dodgson ('Lewis Carroll'), a close friend of the MacDonalds, noted in his diary (February 10, 1863) that he had just finished reading the novel, and discussed it with the author, who told him that Falconer was 'an ideal character'.

Following on from *The Portent*, the supernatural is again dealt with. According to Joseph Johnson (*George MacDonald*, 1906, p.226) this element was responsible for much of the popular interest in the book.

MacDonald experienced great difficulty in getting it published.

> 'Smith, Elder & Co. found *David Elginbrod* hardly more attractive than *Seekers and Finders*. Their verdict coincided with every publisher's in London. . . . Had it not been for the daughter of a Manchester friend . . . the book might never have been published. [She] asked if she might show it to her friend, Miss Mulock. . . . The authoress of *John Halifax, Gentleman* at once realised the book's merits, and took it to her own publishers, Hurst and Blackett, and told them they were fools to refuse it. "Are we?" they asked. "Then of course we will print it without delay." They gave its author £90. . . . Never again had he difficulty in placing a book' (*Life*, p.322).

Ruskin, another close friend, found it 'full of noble things and with beautiful little sentences . . . it is a little too subtle in some places for a story, I think, but very beautiful elsewhere' (*Life*, p.323, quoting one of Ruskin's earliest letters to MacDonald, dated June 30, 1863).

(? 1871) Published in one volume by Hurst and Blackett, 8vo, pp.vi, 412, with frontispiece by Edward Hughes (steel engraving).

1871 Published as vols.1189 and 1190 of Tauchnitz's *Collection of British Authors*, Leipzig: pp.326, 311.

1872 First American publication. Published by Loring, Boston.

1879 Published in Munro's *Seaside Library*, New York.

[189?] Published by Routledge, New York.

1897 Published as no.14 of the Lavender Series; Fenno, New York.

1900 Published by Hurst and Blackett.

1906 Published by Hurst and Blackett sixpenny edition.

1917 Published by Burt, New York, in Home Library Series.

1921 Published by Hurst and Blackett.

(n.d.: before 1925) Published by Lothrop, Boston; Mackay, Philadelphia; and Winston, Philadelphia.

1927 Published by Cassell.

1863

15. TELL US A STORY. A fairy story, published in the *Illustrated London News*, December 19, 1863, with two illustrations by C. Robinson.

Reprinted as 'The Giant's Heart' in *Adela Cathcart* (1864), *Dealings with the Fairies* (1867), and *Works of Fancy and Imagination* (1871). For further reprints see *Dealings with the Fairies*.

1864

16. 'THE WOW O' RIVVEN.' This story first appeared in *Good Words*, Feb. 1864, pp.153–9, with an illustration of the fool.

MacDonald described the setting (the church of Ruthven, Aberdeen-shire, which he visited for the first time in 1891) in a letter to his wife:

'Right at the foot of the belfry the fool of my story is buried, with a gravestone set up by the people of Huntly telling about him, and how he thought that bell, now above his body, always said "Come hame, come hame" ' (*Life*, p.521).

1864　Reprinted as 'The Bell: A Sketch in Pen and Ink', in the first edition of *Adela Cathcart*, vol.I, pp.241–75.

1868　Published separately as 'The Wow o' Rivven, or the Idiot's Home'.

1871　Reprinted in *Works of Fancy and Imagination*, vol.X.

[1909]　Reprinted in *The Portent and other stories*, published by Fisher, Unwin (see under *The Portent*, 1864).

1973　Reprinted in the Eerdmans/Mowbray collection (see under *The Gifts of the Child Christ*, 1882).

1864

17. ADELA CATHCART. By George MacDonald, M.A. Quota-tion from Chaucer's *Man of Lawes Tale*. Hurst and Blackett, [April] 1864.

8vo. 3 vols: vol.I, pp.viii, 324: vol.II, pp.vi, 320: vol.III, pp.vi, 360, (8 adv.). Dark brown cloth. Dedicated to John Rutherford Russell [physician to the Homoeopathic Hospital].

This book is really a setting for a number of fairy tales, parables and poems, some of which had already appeared in periodicals; the framework is that of a 'story-telling club'. The *Athenaeum* of May 7,

ADELA CATHCART

BY

GEORGE MAC DONALD M.A.

AUTHOR OF

"DAVID ELGINBROD,"

&c., &c.

Me list not of the chaf ne of the stre
Maken so long a tale as of the corn.
CHAUCER.—*Man of Lawes Tale.*

IN THREE VOLUMES.

VOL. I.

LONDON:
HURST AND BLACKETT, PUBLISHERS,
SUCCESSORS TO HENRY COLBURN,
13, GREAT MARLBOROUGH STREET.
1864.
The right of Translation is reserved.

2. Title page of the first edition of *Adela Cathcart*.

So I did begin—

"Title: THE LIGHT PRINCESS.

"Second Title: A FAIRY-TALE WITHOUT FAIRIES."

"Author: JOHN SMITH, Gentleman.

"Motto:—'Your Servant, Goody Gravity.'

"From—SIR CHARLES GRANDISON."

"I must be very stupid, I fear, Mr. Smith; but to tell the truth, *I* can't make head or tail of it," said Mrs. Cathcart.

"Give me leave, madam," said I; "that is my office. Allow me, and I hope to make both head and tail of it for you. But let me give you first a more general, and indeed a more applicable motto for my story. It is this—from no worse authority than John Milton:

'Great bards beside
In sage and solemn times have sung
Of turneys and of trophies hung;
Of forests and inchantments drear,
Where more is meant than meets the ear.'

"Milton here refers to Spenser in particu-

lar, most likely. But what distinguishes the true bard in such work is, that *more is meant than meets the ear*; and although I am no bard, I should scorn to write anything that only spoke to the *ear*, which signifies the sur-face understanding."

General silence followed, and I went on.

"THE LIGHT PRINCESS.

"CHAPTER I.—WHAT! NO CHILDREN?

"Once upon a time, so long ago, that I have quite forgotten the date, there lived a king and queen who had no children.

"And the king said to himself: 'All the queens of my acquaintance have children, some three, some seven, and some as many as twelve; and my queen has not one. I feel ill-used.' So he made up his mind to be cross with his wife about it. But she bore it all like a good patient queen as she was. Then the king grew very cross indeed. But

3.   First appearance of 'The Light Princess' in Volume 1 of *Adela Cathcart*.

1864, criticised the author for having ransacked his desk for 'old bits of writing he had in his possession'. The phrase 'more is meant than meets the ear' occurs on p.123 of vol.I – it was to be used as the motto to *Dealings with Fairies*, 1867.

The following are here given in order of appearance in the book: only those marked with an asterisk were included in the second edition (1882):

Vol.I　★Translation of a Christmas hymn by Luther in eleven stanzas, beginning 'From heaven above I come to you'.
　　　　'The Light Princess'
　　　　'The Bell: A Sketch in Pen and Ink'
　　　★'Birth, Dreaming and Death'

Vol.II　★'The Curate and his Wife'
　　　　'The Shadows'
　　　　'The Broken Swords'
　　　★'My Uncle Peter' (part 1)

Vol.III　★'My Uncle Peter' (concluded)
　　　　'The Giant's Heart'
　　　★'The Two Gordons' (a Scots ballad)
　　　★'A Child's Holiday'
　　　　'The Cruel Painter'
　　　　'The Castle: A Parable'

'The Broken Swords' first appeared in 1854 (q.v.), 'The Giant's Heart' in 1863 as 'Tell Us a Story' (q.v.); and 'The Bell' in February, 1864 as 'The Wow o' Rivven' in *Good Words* (q.v.). 'The Light Princess', 'The Giant's Heart', and 'The Shadows' were reprinted in *Dealings with the Fairies*, 1867 (q.v.).

[1875?]　First American publication. Published by Loring, Boston.

1882　Second edition, published by Sampson Low, Marston, Searle and Rivington, in one vol: 8vo, pp.iv, 412. This drastically-revised edition was 'hurried through the press without MacDonald's seeing the proofs' (Bulloch, p.11). It included the following, which did not appear in the 1864 edition: 'The Lost Lamb' and 'The Snow Fight' (both in ch.XV), and 'An Invalid's Winter' (a parable, ch.XX). 'The Snow Fight' first appeared in *Good Words for the Young*, Nov./Dec., 1872.

1882　Published in Munro's *Seaside Library*, New York.

1890, 1894　Published by Sampson Low.

1905　Published by George Newnes: pp.416.

1908　Published by Edwin Dalton from the Newnes plates.

[1911] Published by McKay, Philadelphia.

1864

18.   THE PORTENT: A STORY OF THE INNER VISION OF THE HIGHLANDERS, COMMONLY CALLED THE SECOND SIGHT. By George MacDonald. [Motto from Donne's *Air and Angels*.] Smith, Elder & Co., 1864.

8vo; pp.viii, 290, (2). Purple cloth. Dedication, (pp.iii–v), in the form of a letter, to Duncan McColl, Esq., RN, Huntly [an uncle of MacDonald's stepmother], dated Kensington, May, 1864, in which the story is described as 'a romance' and 'a day-dream'. The illustration of 1860 is omitted (see no.10).

Greville MacDonald says of it:

> 'The story is different from almost any other of his books, but it at once convinced friends and publishers of his art in simple narrative. It deals with the Highland belief in second-sight – of which gift my father would reluctantly admit he had himself no trace. It is weird, yet strangely convincing, and has no touch of the didactic. My mother once told an admirer, that when she asked my father for the story's meaning, he said, "You may make of it what you like. If you see anything in it, take it and I am glad you have it; but I wrote it for the tale." Its author received forty pounds for its serial use, and thirty for the copyright of the book' (*Life*, p.318, which also gives, on p.293, the sole recorded instance of 'second sight' in MacDonald's family).

A note on p.ii states that the book is 'a portion reprinted from the Cornhill Magazine and completed'. The 1860 version of some 20,000 words was extended to about 30,000, and divided into 27 chapters, of which ch.7 (pp.79–86) is new, as is all after p.173. There are also further additions and revisions of the 1860 text. But most important of all – and neither Bulloch nor Greville MacDonald comment on this – is the complete change in the direction and ending of the story. The tale, related in the first person by Duncan, a young tutor, concerns his love for Lady Alice, who has some mysterious mental condition and is somnambulistic; he meets her in the house of Lord Hilton whose younger children he is tutoring. He hears the sound of a clanking horse-shoe (a personal omen of ill-fortune) and is later turned out of the house when his nocturnal meetings with Lady Alice are discovered. He enlists, is wounded at Waterloo, and takes to wandering in a vain search for Lady Alice. There the first version ends, but in the 1864 version he returns, after 12 years, to the almost-deserted house of the Hiltons to find that Lady Alice is still there. They elope and marry, Lady Alice's mental condition is cured, and all ends happily. This is completely at variance with the earlier chapters: however, the story is of considerable significance both autobiographically and from the point of view of MacDonald's evolution as a writer.

Joseph Johnson noted that 'Lady Alice, the somnambulist, is the first of many characters, beset with a form of mental or nervous disease, that appear in other stories' (*George MacDonald*, 1906, p.228). This was, in itself, a 'portent', since, for the last five years of his life, MacDonald lapsed into a mysterious mental state which has never been satisfactorily diagnosed – and we must furthermore note that MacDonald himself, like Lady Alice, was a step-child.

We also have, in the 1864 version, significant echoes of that old library, which has never been identified, the books of which MacDonald catalogued during a summer vacation while a student, and which exercised such a powerful influence on his imagination. 'I found in the library . . . many romances of a very marvellous sort . . . and a whole nest of the German classics . . .' (p.83). Duncan shows Lady Alice four stanzas of a poem by 'Von Salis' [J. G. von Salis-Seewis], 'Psyche's Sorrow' [1793], which he has translated from the German (p.161): the full nine stanzas appeared as 'Psyche's Mourning' in *Exotics*, 1876. A quotation from Novalis – 'Our life is not a dream, but it may become one, and perhaps ought to become one.' – was to be used again, in a slightly revised form, over thirty years later, to end his last major work, *Lilith*.

1871   Reprinted in *Works of Fancy and Imagination*, vol.vii.

1885   First American publication. Published in Munro's *Seaside Library*, New York, and in the pocket edition of same.

1902   Published by Munro, New York: 12mo, pp.75.

[1909]   Published by Fisher, Unwin, in the *Adelphi Library*, as *The Portent and other stories*: pp.xii, 275, (1). The other stories are 'The Cruel Painter'; 'The Castle'; 'The Wow o' Rivven'; 'The Broken Swords'; 'The Gray Wolf'; and 'Uncle Cornelius His Story'.

[n.d.]   Published by Loring, Portland, Maine.

[1911]   Published by McKay, Philadelphia, with *Phantastes*.

1924   Centenary Edition. This is the edition of [1909] reissued in off-white cloth and gilt, with a reduced facsimile of MacDonald's bookplate on the front cover in brown. There is no publisher's imprint, the title page states simply 'CENTENARY/EDITION/ 1824–1924'. It was never published but presented to guests at the Conversazione held in London on Dec. 10, 1924 (see Appendix F).

1864

19.   AN INVALID'S WINTER IN ALGERIA. MacDonald's account of his visit appeared in *Good Words*, Oct. 1864, pp.793–9, with one illustration (a view of Algiers).

The MacDonalds left for Algiers in Oct., 1856, and returned in April, 1857. The *Life* devotes a chapter to the Algerian visit, but does not record this article.

1865

20.   ALEC FORBES OF HOWGLEN. By George MacDonald, M.A. [Motto from Wordsworth's Second Evening Voluntary.] Hurst & Blackett, 1865.

8vo: 3 vols: vol.I, pp.vi, 304; vol.II, pp.iv, 300; vol.III, pp.iv, 300, (14 adv.). Light-red cloth, gilt spine, plain edges. Reviewed in the *Athenaeum*, June 17, 1865.

This novel was originally to have been called *The Little Grey Town*, but the title was rejected by the publishers as 'not conforming to the then fashionable nomenclature in Fiction' (*Life*, p.19). It is largely autobiographical, relating to Huntly, Aberdeenshire, where MacDonald was born: he spent his boyhood at Upper Pirriesmill, the 'Howglen' of the novel. 'Murdoch Malison' was MacDonald's schoolmaster, the Rev. C. S. – 'a man with quite a savage sense of duty' (*Life*, p.60: further identifications are given on pp.25, 53, 113).

Lewis Carroll recorded in his diary (Jan. 16, 1866) that he found the story very enjoyable, and the character of Annie Anderson one of the most delightful in fiction. 'The Scotch dialect, too, is pleasant enough when one gets a little used to it.'

1865   Published as vols.801 and 802 of Tauchnitz's *Collection of British Authors*, Leipzig. 8vo, pp.iv, 339 and pp.iv, 335.

[1867] Published by Hurst & Blackett in 1 vol: 8vo, pp.440, (4 adv.), with frontispiece by Arthur Hughes, steel-engraved by J. Saddler, dated 15 June, 1867. Green cloth, gilt spine, blind-stamped covers. Printed by John Childs and Son.

[?1868]   As above, but slightly later. Printed by Clay and Taylor, Bungay.

1872   First American publication. Published by Harper, New York.

1880   Published by Munro, New York (*Seaside Library*).

[?1891]   Published by Routledge, New York.

1900   Published by Hurst & Blackett.

1901   Published by Hurst & Blackett, sixpenny edition.

1911   Published by McKay, Philadelphia.

1921   Published by Hurst & Blackett.

1927   Published by Cassell (reprint of edition of 1900).

1865

21.   ANNALS OF A QUIET NEIGHBOURHOOD. Serialised as 'by the vicar' in the *Sunday Magazine*, October, 1865–September, 1866. With eight woodcut illustrations by Robert Barnes, three by William Small, and one headpiece by T. Salmon.

The 'quiet neighbourhood' is based on Arundel, where MacDonald was Congregationalist minister from 1850 to 1853. The story was published in book form at the end of 1866 (dated 1867, q.v.).

1865

22.   A JOURNEY REJOURNEYED. By George MacDonald. *The Argosy*, Dec., 1865–Jan., 1866, pp.53–63, 127–33. An account, in conversational form, of a visit to Switzerland.

George MacDonald spent a holiday in Switzerland in the summer of 1865 (see *Life*, pp.347–52).

1866

23.   THE FAIRY FLEET – AN ENGLISH MÄRCHEN. By George MacDonald. *The Argosy*, April, 1866, pp.417–32.

This story begins as a continuation of *A Journey Rejourneyed* (no.22):

'DEAR MR. EDITOR – I thank you kindly for printing James's talk about the Alps.'

James then goes on to tell a fairy story which he does not complete ('I only want to keep the end of my yarn free that I may splice it afterwards if I like'). The yarn was indeed spliced afterwards – without the desultory help of James – with 'The Fairy Cobbler' (no.33) to form 'The Carasoyn', which first appeared in vol.IX of *Works of Fancy and Imagination*, 1871.

1866

24. NEW TRANSLATIONS OF SOME GERMAN HYMNS. 'By the author of "Annals of a Quiet Neighbourhood".' *Sunday Magazine*. Oct., 1866, pp.30–32.

Four hymns, one each by Gerhardt, Hans Sachs, Luther, and one anonymous.

The Luther hymn appeared with revisions in *The Sunday Magazine*, Sept. 1, 1867 as 'Simeon the Patriarch's Song of Praise', and with further revisions in *Exotics*, 1876, pp.109, 110.

1866

25. PORT IN A STORM. A story which first appeared in *Argosy*, Nov., 1866. Reprinted in *The Gifts of the child Christ*, 1882.

1866–67

26. LUTHER THE SINGER. 'By the author of "Annals of a Quiet Neighbourhood".' *Sunday Magazine*, Dec. 1, 1866– Sept. 1, 1867; pp.149–51, 255–7, 331–2, 387–9, 449–51, 570–2, 681–2, 840–1, +2 woodcut illustrations facing pp.150, 256.

Translation of Luther's Song Book, with a 'Prologue by the Translator' and interspersed commentaries. The prologue and songs were reprinted with some revisions in *Exotics*, 1876. The commentaries were omitted. The titles, in chronological order, are:

Prologue by the Translator, pp.149–50, Dec. 1, 1866,
Dame Music, p.150, Dec. 1, 1866,
Advent, pp.150–1, Dec. 1, 1866,
Christmas, p.151, Dec. 1, 1866,
A Song of Praise for the Birth of Our Lord Jesus Christ, p.151, Dec. 1, 1866,
A Song of the Child Jesus, for children at Christmas, p.256, Jan. 1, 1867,
A Song concerning the Two Martyrs of Christ, burnt at Brussels by the Lions of Sophists, which took place in the year 1523, pp.256–7, Jan. 1, 1867,
Epiphany, p.331, Feb. 1, 1867,
Easter, pp.331–2, Feb. 1, 1867,
A Song of Praise at Easter, p.332, Feb. 1, 1867,
Pentecost, pp.387–8, March 1, 1867,
A Song of Praise, p.388, March 1, 1867,

The Trinity, p.388, March 1, 1867,

The Twelfth Psalm, p.449, April 1, 1867,

The Fourteenth Psalm, p.450, April 1, 1867,

The Forty-sixth Psalm, p.450, April 1, 1867,

The Hundred and Twenty-fourth Psalm, p.450, April 1, 1867,

A Child's Song, to sing against the Two Arch-enemies of Christ and his Holy church, the Pope and the Turks, p.450, April 1, 1867,

A Song of the Holy Christian Church, from the Twelfth Chapter of the Apocalypse, pp.450–1, April 1, 1867. On p.570, May 1, 1867, Mac-Donald wrote:

> 'I am much indebted to an unknown correspondent of the Editor of this Magazine, for pointing out that a good many of these Hymns of Luther are translations of old Latin Hymns.'

He then gives one verse in Latin beginning 'Egressus ejus a Patre', a translation of that verse in English, and his translation from Luther. He also expressed the hope of printing the Latin originals along with the German and English translations: this hope was unfulfilled.

The Sixty-seventh Psalm, p.570, May 1, 1867,

The Hundred and twenty-eighth Psalm, p.570, May 1, 1867,

A Song of Thanksgiving for the Kindness so Great which God hath shown to us in Christ, pp.570–1, May 1, 1867,

The Commandments, p.571, May 1, 1867,

The Creed, pp.571–2, May 1, 1867,

The Lord's Prayer, plainly set forth, and turned into metre, p.681, July 1, 1867,

The Litany, pp.681–2, July 1, 1867,

Baptism, p.682, July 1, 1867,

Repentance: The Hundred and Thirtieth Psalm, p.682, July 1, 1867,

A Song of St. John Huss, improved by Dr. Mart. Luther, p.840, Sept. 1, 1867,

A Song of Praise, p.840, Sept. 1, 1867,

Death, p.840, Sept. 1, 1867,

Simeon the Patriarch's Song of Praise, pp.840–1, Sept. 1, 1867,

The Praise of God, p.841, Sept. 1, 1867,

The Song of Praise, 'Te Deum Laudamus', turned into German by Dr. Mart. Luther, p.841, Sept. 1, 1867,

Of Life at Court, p.841, Sept. 1, 1867.

1866

27. THE HISTORY OF ROBERT FALCONER. Serialised anonymously in *Argosy*, Dec. 1866–Nov. 1867, with 14 illustrations by William Small.

A footnote to ch. VII states that none of the poems in the story are by the author, though they are his property and appear in print for the first time. On the last page appeared the note: 'This history will be published with fuller details, rendered impossible here for want of space, in the coming spring.'

When the instalments began to appear, MacDonald's uncle James wrote to him protesting that many of the characters were portraits drawn from life, and would give offence. Furthermore he drove his gig post-haste to the editor of the *Banffshire Journal*, warning him against reviewing the story. 'As far as I can ascertain he succeeded,' noted Greville McDonald (*Life*, p.242).

MacDonald wrote to the *Athenaeum* (August 1, 1868) complaining that 'one of the principal libraries was supplying as "Robert Falconer" the monthly parts, cut out of *Argosy* and bound by themselves.' The story appeared in book form in June, 1868 (q.v.), much revised and enlarged, and was further enlarged *c*.1895.

1867

28. ANNALS OF A QUIET NEIGHBOURHOOD. By George Mac-Donald, M.A. Hurst & Blackett, 1867 [1866].

8vo: 3 vols: vol.I, pp.vi, 386: vol.II, pp.vi, 321: vol.III, pp.vi, 276, (16 adv. dated Oct. 1866). Green cloth, gilt spine, plain edges.

Serialised in the *Sunday Magazine*, in the year commencing Oct., 1865 (q.v.). Reviewed in the *British Quarterly Review*, Jan., 1867. Some associations with Arundel are given in the *Life*, pp.154, 155.

1867 Published in one vol. by Hurst & Blackett.

1867 Published in two vols. by Tauchnitz, Leipzig. (*Collection of English Authors*, nos.881, 882).

1867 First American publication. Published by Harper, New York (12mo, pp.381).

1867 Published by Strahan, pp.vi, 590.

1872 Published by Strahan, pp.vi, 590.

1873 Published by Lothrop, Boston, and by Routledge, New York.

1874   Published by W. Isbister.

1877   Published by Daldy, Isbister.

1879   Published by Munro, New York ('Seaside Library').

1884   Published by Kegan, Paul.

1886   Published by Strahan.

[189?] Published by Routledge, New York.

1892   Published by Kegan, Paul.

1893   Published by Kegan, Paul, pp. vi, 590.

1895   Published by Harper, New York ('Franklin Square Library')

1901   Published by Kegan, Paul.

[1911] Published by McKay, Philadelphia.

1867

29.   UNSPOKEN SERMONS. By George MacDonald. Alexander Strahan, 1867. [1866].

8vo: pp. viii, 245, (3). Blue cloth, gilt spine ('George MacDonald, MA'), Strahan's anchor device in gilt on front cover: plain edges. On the title page is printed in red Ἔπεα Ἄπτερα ('Wingless Words') and [motto] 'Comfort ye, comfort ye my people'. [Dedication, p. v.] – 'These Ears of Corn, gathered and rubbed in my hands upon broken Sabbaths, I offer first to my Wife, and then to my other Friends'.

This is the first of a series of three collections of *Unspoken Sermons*, the others being published in 1885 and 1889. There are 12 sermons, all on New Testament texts: (1) The Child in the Midst; (2) The Consuming Fire; (3) The Higher Faith; (4) It Shall Not Be Forgiven; (5) The New Name; (6) The Heart and the Treasure; (7) The Temptation in the Wilderness; (8) The Eloi; (9) The Hands of the Father; (10) Love thy Neighbour; (11) Love thine Enemy; (12) The God of the Living. Reviewed in the *British Quarterly Review*, April, 1867.

1869   Published by Strahan ('Third Edition').

1874   Published by Daldy, Isbister, 'Fifth Edition'.

1884   Published by Strahan.

[*c*.1890]   Published by Routledge, New York.

[*c*.1890]   Published by Longmans.

1867

30. GUILD COURT: A LONDON STORY. Serialised in *Good Words*. Jan.–June, 1867, with 12 woodcuts by G. J. Pinwell. Published in book form in 1867, dated 1868 (q.v.).

1867

31. DEALINGS WITH THE FAIRIES. By George MacDonald. Alexander Strahan, 1867.

Given as 32mo in the publishers ad, and as 16mo in the British Library General Catalogue. The view of the British Library, as expressed in a letter to the compiler, is that this divergence is a matter of 'doctors differ'. Pp.x, 308 (4 adv. dated Dec., 1866). Green cloth, decorated in gilt and black: all edges gilt. Price 2s. 6d. Motto: 'Where more is meant than meets the ear' [Milton]. Frontispiece plus 11 page illustrations by Arthur Hughes. Contents: (1) 'The Light Princess'; (2) 'The Giant's Heart'; (3) 'The Shadows'; (4) 'Cross Purposes'; (5) 'The Golden Key'. The Preface (p.vii) is here given in full:

'MY CHILDREN,
You know I do not tell you stories as some papas do. Therefore I give you a book of stories. You have read them all before except the last. But you have not seen Mr. Hughes' drawings before.
If plenty of children like this volume, you shall have another soon.
YOUR PAPA.'

'The Light Princess' and 'The Shadows' first appeared in *Adela Cathcart*, 1864. 'The Giant's Heart' was first published as 'Tell us a Story' in the Christmas number of *The Illustrated London News*, Dec., 1863, and was reprinted as 'The Giant's Heart' in *Adela Cathcart*, 1864. 'Cross Purposes: A Fairy Tale' appeared in *Beeton's Christmas Annual*, 1862, pp.58–63, signed George MacDonald, making it the earliest of his fairy tales to be published. 'The Golden Key' appears in print for the first time.

The five stories in this collection have often been reprinted, sometimes singly, but, more frequently, in collections including later stories, and under various titles. (See no.44, vols VIII and IX.)

1868 and 1890   *Dealings with the Fairies*. Published by Strahan; square 16mo.

[1890] *The Light Princess and other fairy stories* ['The Giant's Heart' and 'The Golden Key']. Published by Blackie; 8vo, pp.192, with three woodcuts by L.L.B. [Leonard Leslie Brooke].

[1890] *Cross Purposes and The Shadows*. Published by Blackie, pp.96.

The Light Princess

AND OTHER FAIRY TALES

BY

GEORGE MACDONALD

ILLUSTRATED BY

MAUD HUMPHREY

G. P. PUTNAM'S SONS
NEW YORK AND LONDON
The Knickerbocker Press

4.   Title page of *The Light Princess and Other Fairy Tales* (1893).

HAT we have in English no word corresponding to the German *Mährchen*, drives us to use the word *Fairytale*, regardless of the fact that the tale may have nothing to do with any sort of fairy. The old use of the word *Fairy*, by Spenser at least, might, however, well be adduced, were justification or excuse necessary where *need must*.

Were I asked, what is a fairytale? I should reply. *Read Undine: that is a fairytale; then read this and that as well, and you will see what is a fairytale.* Were I further begged to describe the *fairytale*, or define what it is, I would make answer, that I should as soon think of describing the abstract human face, or stating what must go to constitute a human being. A fairytale is just a fairytale, as a face is just a face; and of all fairytales I know, I think Undine the most beautiful.

Many a man, however, who would not attempt to define *a man*, might venture to say something as to

5. First publication of an essay by GMD on the nature of the fairy tale appearing as the Preface to an American edition of *The Light Princess and Other Fairy Tales* (1893).

1891   First American publication. *Dealings with the Fairies*. Published by Routledge, New York; 16mo.

[1893] *The Light Princess and other fairy tales*. Published by G. P. Putnam's Sons, New York; 8vo, pp.xiv, 305. Contains: (i) 'The Light Princess'; (ii) 'The Giant's Heart'; (iii) 'The Shadows'; (iv) 'Cross Purposes'; (v) 'The Golden Key'; (vi) 'The Carasoyn'; (vii) 'Little Daylight'. Illustrated by Maud Humphrey (mother of Humphrey Bogart). Cover decorated with pictorial design in black on buff cloth.

Contains two stories not included in *Dealings with the Fairies*, and an introduction in which MacDonald gives his views on the nature of the fairy tale; this was published as an essay entitled 'The Fantastic Imagination' in *A Dish of Orts* (q.v.), also published in 1893. In the preface to *A Dish of Orts*, dated Aug. 5, 1893, MacDonald wrote:

> 'The paper on "The Fantastic Imagination" had its origin in the repeated request of readers for an explanation of things in certain shorter stories I had written. It forms the preface to an American edition of my so-called Fairy Tales.'

'The Carasoyn' first appeared in its complete form in *Works of Fancy and Imagination*, 1871 (q.v.).
'Little Daylight' was originally part of *At the Back of the North Wind* (1871), and was published separately in *Works of Fancy and Imagination*.

1904   *Fairy Tales by George MacDonald*, edited and with an introduction by Greville MacDonald. Published by Arthur C. Fifield. With 13 illustrations and title page by Arthur Hughes. Contains the seven stories of Putnam's 1893 edition, plus 'The Day Boy and the Night Girl', which first appeared as 'The History of Photogen and Nycteris: a Day and Night Märchen', in the Christmas number of *The Graphic*, 1879.

1905–1906 The above, issued by Fifield in five sixpenny parts: (i) 'The Light Princess'; (ii) 'The Giant's Heart' and 'The Golden Key'; (iii) 'The Shadows' and 'Little Daylight'; (iv) 'Cross Purposes' and 'The Carasoyn'; (v) 'The Day Boy and the Night Girl'.

1905   *The Light Princess*. Published by Burt, New York, in the 'St. Nicholas' series.

1906   *The Golden Key*. Published by the T. Y. Crowell, New York.

[1907] *Cross Purposes and The Shadows*. Published by Blackie, with col. frontispiece by H. M. Brock; pp.96.

[1913] *Fairy Tales* ['The Golden Key and 'Cross Purposes']. Published in English by Carl Winter, Heidelberg; small 8vo; pp.iv, 96, with 6 coloured plates by Paul Scheurich.

1915　*The Light Princess.* Crowell's 'Child Life' series, New York: pp.74, illustrated.

1920　*Fairy Tales by George MacDonald.* Reissue of the 1904 Fifield edition, published by George Allen & Unwin.

1924　The above, published as a centenary edition. 'The Day Boy and the Night Girl' appears under its original title of 'Photogen and Nycteris'.

1925　*The Light Princess.* Published by Blackie; illustrated.

1926　*The Light Princess.* Published by Macmillan, New York; illustrated by Dorothy P. Lathrop.

[1928] *The Light Princess.* 'The Giant's Heart', 'The Golden Key', 'Cross Purposes'. Published by Blackie, pp.232, with 4 col. plates by F. D. Bedford.

[1946] 'Cross Purposes', with illustrations by Muriel Gill; included in *The Favourite Wonder Book*, published by Odhams Press.

1961　'*The Light Princess and other tales*: being the complete [sic] fairy stories of George MacDonald.' Published by Victor Gollancz. With 16 illustrations by Arthur Hughes and an introduction by Roger Lancelyn Green. Contains the 8 stories of the Fifield edition of 1904. Reprinted 1972, 1973.

1961　As above, published by Watts, New York.

[1962] *The Light Princess.* Published by Crowell, New York; illustrated by William Pène du Bois.

1967　*The Light Princess.*

1972　*The Golden Key.*
　　　　Two companion volumes, published by Farrar, Straus and Giroux, New York, in 1967, and by The Bodley Head, London, in 1972. Illustrations and jacket designs by Maurice Sendak. *The Golden Key* has an afterword by W. H. Auden (pp.81–6) dated Dec., 1966. A footnote referring to the author's indebtedness to Novalis for certain geometrical figures described in the text, is transferred from p.60 to the last page but one (p.87).

1972　*Evenor* [Reprints of 'The Wise Woman', 'The Carasoyn', and 'The Golden Key'.] Published by Pan/Ballantine as the third Mac-Donald item in their 'Adult Fantasy' series. Paperback, pp.xiv, 210; dedicated to C. S. Lewis. Introduction ('The Dubious Land') by Lin Carter, in which he explains his choice of the title as originating in Plato ('Evenor, the Earth-born').

> 'MacDonald sees terrestrial nature as a maternal or paternal figure, and his stories, which contain numerous enigmatic and mysterious figures of divine authority, almost seem to share this element of Platonic mysticism' (pp. xiii, xiv).

The collection is prefaced by six lines from 'A Hidden Life'.

1973   The 8 stories of the 1904 Fifield edition, included in the Eerdmans/Mowbray collection – see under 'The Gifts of the Child Christ', 1882.

1973 and 1974   'The Golden Key' and 'The Day Boy and the Night Girl'; included in *Beyond the Looking-Glass: Extraordinary Works of Fairy Tale and Fantasy*, published by Stonehill Publishing Co., New York, in 1973, and by Hart-Davis, MacGibbon, in 1974. Edited and with an introduction by Jonathan Cott. With 3 photographs of MacDonald and his family, and 2 illustrations by Arthur Hughes.

1867

32.   THE SEABOARD PARISH. Serialised in *The Sunday Magazine*, Oct., 1867–Aug., 1868, with illustrations by J. Gordon Thomson. Published in book form in 1868 (q.v.). A sequel to *Annals of a Quiet Neighbourhood*.

1867

33.   THE FAIRY COBBLER. By George MacDonald. Published in *Good Cheer*, Dec. 25, 1867, with a woodcut illustration by A. Houghton.

This was to form the second part of 'The Carasoyn' in *Works of Fancy and Imagination* (q.v. 1871) – the first part had already appeared as 'The Fairy Fleet' (q.v. 1866).

1867

34.   THE DISCIPLE AND OTHER POEMS. By George Mac-Donald. Strahan & Co., 1867 [1868].

8vo: pp. viii, 332, (4 adv. dated Jan. 1868). Dark-brown cloth speckled with red; blind-stamped; front cover has a gilt ornament in each corner, and Strahan's anchor device in gilt in the centre. Gilt spine, plain edges.

Contents: 'The Disciple', pp.3–49. 'Songs of the Days and Nights' (8 groups of poems), pp.53–84. 'Parables' (9 poems), pp.87–162. 'Roadside Poems' (6 poems), pp.165–86. 'Organ Songs' (22 poems), pp.189–237. 'Violin Songs' (7 poems), pp.241–53. 'For Children' (5 poems), pp.257–74. 'Ballads' (3 poems), pp.277–86. 'Scotch Songs and Ballads' (10 poems), pp.289–330. 'To A.I.N.B.' [Lady Byron], p.331. 'To Garibaldi', p.332. Reviewed in *The Athenaeum*, April 4, 1868.

'The Disciple', to which the *Life* devotes one chapter, is autobiographical, relating to MacDonald's last year at Aberdeen University.

1868   Second edition, published by Strahan. (For reprints see *Works of Fancy and Imagination*, 1871, and *The Poetical Works*, 1893.)

1868

35.   GUILD COURT. By George MacDonald, M.A. Hurst & Blackett, 1868 [1867].

8vo: 3 vols: vol.I, pp.vi, 320; vol.II, pp.vi, 317, (1); vol.III, pp.vi, 302, (18 adv.). Ochre cloth, gilt spine, plain edges.

Serialised as 'Guild Court, a London story', in *Good Words*, Jan.–Dec., 1867 (q.v.).

1868   Published by Harper, New York.

1881   Published by Sampson Low, and in Munro's 'Seaside Library', New York.

1891   Published by Sampson Low.

1905   Published by Newnes, pp.396.

1908   Published by Edwin Dalton from the Newnes plates.

[1911] Published by McKay, Philadelphia.

1868

36.   ROBERT FALCONER. By George MacDonald, LLD. [Motto from a speech by Brutus in *Julius Caesar*.] Hurst & Blackett, 1868.

8vo: 3 vols: vol.I – pp.vi, 326, (2); vol.II – pp.vi, 303, (1); vol.III – pp.vi, 306, (18 adv.). Purple cloth, gilt spine, plain edges.

Dedication: 'To the memory of the man who stands highest in the oratory of my memory, Alexander John Scott, I, daring, presume to dedicate this book.' Scott (1805–66) was first principal of Owen's

College, Manchester, and had a great influence on MacDonald: the *Life* devotes a chapter to him (pp. 191–5).

This is a revised and greatly extended version of 'The History of Robert Falconer', which was serialised in *Argosy*, Dec., 1866–Nov., 1867. A note on p.iv repeats the statement that appeared in the serialised version, that none of the poems are by the author, and adds that they were 'the careless work of a friend of his boyhood' – in fact, his brother John Hill MacDonald (d. 1858), who appears in the story as 'Eric Ericson' (*Life*, p. 164).

The novel is largely autobiographical. Falconer was the name of Mac-Donald's maternal grandmother, but 'Mrs. Falconer' of the story was based on his paternal grandmother, Mrs. Charles Edward MacDonald, born in Huntly in 1756: her portrait appears in the *Life*, p. 25. The story was further enlarged in an undated edition, *c.*1895 (see below).

[*c.*1870] Published by Hurst & Blackett: 8vo, pp.vi, 417, (1), (4 adv.), with a steel-engraved frontispiece of 'The Angel Unawares'. Green cloth, gilt spine, plain edges. Printed by Bradbury, Agnew & Co., Whitefriars. There is a note concerning authorship of the poems, as above, but no table of contents.

[1876] First American publication. Published by Loring, Boston. 12mo, pp.524, with a portrait.

[*c.*1880] Published by Hurst & Blackett – details as for [*c.*1870], with the following changes: binding – black cloth, gilt spine and front cover; advertisements – pp.14; printers – Richard Clay & Sons, London and Bungay.

1881 Published by Munro, New York ('Seaside Library').

[*c.*1895] *New and Enlarged Edition*. Published by Hurst & Blackett. 8vo, pp.viii, 476, (12 adv.), with steel-engraved frontispiece of 'The Angel Unawares'. Binding and printers as for [*c.*1880]. There is now a table of contents (pp.vii, viii), with two additional chapters to Part II, and four to Part III. The note concerning authorship of poems has been amended to read '. . . not a poem in this tale is of his own composition except the last'. This is of seven 4-line stanzas, beginning 'Twilight is near and the day grows old;' – it forms the greater part of a short additional chapter.

According to Greville MacDonald, this poem was never published but was distributed as a Christmas present by his father in 1893 – it appears on pp.314, 315 of *Reminiscences of a Specialist*, headed 'Christmas, 1893', signed 'GMD', and begins 'Twilight is near and the days grow old;' – it is in fact a variant of the *Robert Falconer* version with the seventh stanza omitted. Though Greville MacDonald was unaware of its appearance in *Robert Falconer*, his publication of the poem makes it clear that this enlarged edition must be later than 1893, since George MacDonald would not have distributed as a Christmas present a poem that had already been published. The British Library does not possess a copy, but one has been seen by the compiler, with a prize label dated March 1896.

[1896] *Abridged edition.* No.26 of 'Penny Popular Novels', ed. W. T. Stead, in the 'Masterpiece Library', published by the 'Review of Reviews' office, 16mo, pp.68, (iv adv.). Preface (p.2), text pp.3–68. Light-blue paper wrappers.

[189?] Published by Routledge, New York.

1900 Published by Hurst & Blackett, pp.484.

1907 Published by Hurst & Blackett, price 6*d*.

[1911] Published by McKay, Philadelphia.

1921 Published by Hurst & Blackett, pp.484.

1927 Published by Cassell, pp.viii, 476.

1868

37. THE WOW O' RIVVEN; OR THE IDIOT'S HOME. By George MacDonald. Edited for the Royal Albert Idiot Asylum, by Dora Greenwell. Strahan & Co., 1868. Price 6*d*. or 5*s*. per dozen.

Issued in paper wrappers with lilac outer surfaces, data from title-page printed on front cover within decorated borders. 8vo: pp.32. Frontispiece of the idiot from *Good Words*, Feb., 1864, in which this story first appeared.

Note on p.[4]: '[Reprinted from ADELA CATHCART by permission of the Author].' Text: pp.5–28. Appeal for the Royal Albert Asylum for Idiots and Imbeciles of the Northern Counties, Lancaster, dated April, 1868: pp.[29,30]. Adv.: pp.[31,32].

This is an unabridged reprint from *Adela Cathcart*, 1864, in which it appeared as 'The Bell: A Sketch in Pen and Ink'. Reprinted as 'The Wow o' Rivven' in *Works of Fancy and Imagination*, 1871; *The Portent and other stories*, [1909] (q.v. 1864); and the Eerdmans/Mowbray collection, 1973 (q.v. *The Gifts of the Child Christ*, 1882).

1868

38. THE SEABOARD PARISH. By George MacDonald, LL.D. Tinsley Brothers, 1868.

8vo: 3 vols: vol.I – pp.viii, 292; vol.II – pp.iv, 264; vol.III – pp.iv, 266, (2). Dark-brown cloth, two gilt ornaments on each cover, connected with gilt bands across spine, the design uniform with that of *The Vicar's Daughter* (1872), plain edges.

Serialised in *The Sunday Magazine*, Oct., 1867–Aug., 1868, it is a sequel to *Annals of a Quiet Neighbourhood*, 1867. Dedication: 'To James Powell, Esq., his grateful and loving son–in–law dedicates this book.'

This story resulted from a holiday which the MacDonald family spent in Bude, Cornwall, in the summer of 1867. The incident of the drowned man was actually witnessed by them, and the storm episode, in which two men leaped from a life-boat on the crest of a wave to the main shrouds of a schooner, was told to MacDonald by a coastguard (*Life*, pp.367–70).

1868   First American publication. Published by Routledge, New York.

1869   Published by Strahan.

1872   Published by Strahan with 'Daldy, Isbister & Co.' on the back cover (Bulloch, p.43).

1872   Published by Routledge, New York, with frontispiece+6 wood-cut illustrations.

1879   Published by Munro ('Seaside Library'), New York.

1884   Published by Strahan.

1886   Published by Kegan, Paul ('4th edition').

1890   Published by Kegan, Paul ('5th edition'); pp.viii, 624, with frontispiece.

[189?] Published by Routledge, New York.

n.d.   Published by Kegan Paul, pp.viii, 624.

1901   Published by Kegan Paul.

[1911] Published by McKay, Philadelphia: illustrated.

1868

39.   ENGLAND'S ANTIPHON. By George MacDonald, LL.D.
Macmillan & Co.

This work was published in two forms:

(i) In three parts, dated Oct., Nov., and Dec., 1868, forming Vol.4 of
The Sunday Library for Household Reading. Issued in buff paper wrappers
printed in black, green and brick-red, dated on the front cover. 8vo:
part I – pp.viii, 112, with two illustrations by Arthur Hughes; part II –
pp.113–224, with one illustration by Hughes; part III – pp.225–332. The
illustrations are full-page, and in sepia.

(ii) In book form, from the same plates as the above, with the Hughes'
illustrations. The title page is in sepia, red and blue, and is undated. 8vo:
pp.viii, 332. Bound in blue cloth, gilt spine. In some copies, the spine
and front cover bear Macmillan's device in gilt, with the words *The
Sunday Library for Household Reading*. The British Museum copy has pale
lemon endpapers: another copy has been seen with brown endpapers and
Burns' label.

The preface begins: 'In this book I have sought to trace the course of our
religious poetry from an early period of our literary history,' and ends:
'Heartily do I throw this my small pebble at the head of the great
Sabbath-breaker *Schism*.' It ranges from the sacred lyrics of the thirteenth
century to Tennyson's *In Memoriam*.

1874   Published by Macmillan. As for 1868, except that the title page
and illustrations are black; the red border is thicker; and it is dated
1874. There can be the same variants in binding as noted in (ii)
above.

n.d. before 1880   Published by Lippincott, Philadelphia: 12mo (Bulloch, p.20).

1868

40.   GOOD WORDS FOR THE YOUNG (1868–72): GOOD THINGS
FOR THE YOUNG OF ALL AGES (1872–7).

The magazine *Good Words for the Young* was published monthly by
Strahan from Nov., 1868 to Nov., 1872. The editor for the first year was
Norman MacLeod: he was succeeded by MacDonald, who remained
editor until the final issue.

According to the *Life* (p.361), MacDonald's salary for his first year of
editorship was £600. However, the magazine was not a financial success,
and for the following two years MacDonald continued editing on a

voluntary basis without remuneration. Strahan thought the failure was due to too much of the 'fairy element'; so MacDonald wrote to his wife in a letter dated Feb. 25, 1871 (*Life*, p.412). Five months later he wrote, again to his wife: '. . I am more and more glad I am [sic] to be rid of the editing . . .' (ibid.).

Evidently MacDonald overcame his feelings, not only at the failure of the magazine, but also concerning antagonisms that arose out of accusations that he refused the contributions of others to make space for his own, for he went on to edit the successor to *Good Words*, published by Henry S. King under the title *Good Things for the Young of All Ages*, 1872–3. MacDonald then gave up the editorship: the magazine was again published by Strahan with another change of title (December, 1874) to *Good Things: A Picturesque Magazine for the Young of All Ages*. This was yet again altered, in its final year of publication, to *Good Things: A Picturesque Magazine for Boys and Girls*.

MacDonald's contributions, with dates of first publication in book form in brackets, are as follows:

To 'Good Words, etc.'

(i)   'At the Back of the North Wind', Nov., 1868–Oct., 1870 (1871).
(ii)   'Ranald Bannerman's Boyhood', Nov., 1869–Oct., 1870 (1871).
(iii)   'Willie's Question', a poem, Nov., 1869–Oct., 1870 (*The Poetical Works*, 1893, vol.ii).
(iv)   'The Princess and the Goblin', Nov., 1870–June 1871 (1872).
(v)   'The History of Gutta-Percha Willie', 1872 (1873).
(vi)   'The Wind and the Moon', a poem, 1872 (*A Threefold Cord*, 1883).
(vii)   'The Foolish Harebell', a poem, 1872 (*A Threefold Cord*, 1883).
(viii) 'The Snow Fight', a short story, 1872 (*Adela Cathcart*, 1882).

To 'Good Things, etc.'

(ix)   'Cottage Songs for Cottage Children', a group of 5 poems, 1874 (*A Threefold Cord*, 1883).
(x)   'A Double Story', Dec., 1874–July, 1875 (published in book form as *The Wise Woman*, 1875).
(xi)   'Three Pairs and One', a poem trans-translated from the German through the Dutch, 1876 (*Exotics*, 1876).
(xii)   'What the Owl knows', a poem, 1876.
(xiii) 'The Seashell', a poem, 1876.
(xiv)   'Morning Hymn', a poem, 1876 (*The Poetical Works*, 1893, vol.i).
(xv)   'The Princess and Curdie', Jan.–June, 1877 (1883).

Items (i), (ii), (iv), (v), (vi), and the first 3 poems of item (ix) were illustrated by Arthur Hughes. Some illustrations by Hughes appeared with item (xv) but were unrelated to the text.

1870

41.   THE MIRACLES OF OUR LORD. By George MacDonald. Strahan & Co., 1870.

8vo: pp.viii, 280, (16 adv. dated Nov., 1870). Purple cloth; covers blindstamped; lettering on spine and Strahan's anchor device on front cover in gilt; plain edges.

Dedication (p.v.): 'To F. D. Maurice honoured of God I humbly offer this book.'

The introduction (pp.1–7) begins: 'I have been requested to write some papers on our Lord's miracles.' The book is in fact another collection of 'Unspoken Sermons', divided into 12 chapters of which the first is the introduction. Miracles are regarded by the author as the workings of God in miniature (p.3); he affirms that once we believe in God, it needs no great power of faith to accept them (p.2). The volume is analysed in Joseph Johnson's *George MacDonald* (1906), pp.160–65.

1870   First American publication. Published by Randolph, New York.

[n.d.]   Published by Lippincott, Philadelphia, and Routledge, New York.

1886   Published by Longmans. [Advertised in Longmans, Green's catalogue, 1897, price 3s. 6d.]

1870

42.   WILFRED CUMBERMEDE: An Autobiographical Story. By George MacDonald. Serialised simultaneously in *St. Paul's*, Nov., 1870–Dec., 1871, and *Scribner's Monthly*, New York, Nov., 1870–March, 1872: seven illustrations by F.A.F. appeared in both.

The editor of *Scribner's Monthly*, Dr. J. G. Holland, was a great admirer of MacDonald's work: he met MacDonald in New York in the winter of 1872.

The story was published in book form in 1871 (dated 1872, q.v.).

1871

43. AT THE BACK OF THE NORTH WIND. By George Mac-
Donald. Strahan, [Dec., 1870], 1871.

8vo: pp,viii, 378, (13 adv.): blue cloth, design in gilt and black based on
illustration from p.301 on front cover: all edges gilt. With 76 illustrations
in the text by Arthur Hughes.

Serialised in *Good Words for the Young*, Nov., 1868–Oct., 1870, this was
MacDonald's first 'long' fairy story to be published in book form. Most
of the poems in it were included, in revised form, in *The Poetical Works*,
1893, vol.2, in the section entitled 'Poems for Children'. 'Little Daylight', a self-contained fairy-tale which forms ch.28, has been included in
some collections of his short stories (see *Dealings with the Fairies*, 1867).

1871　First American publication. Published by Routledge, New York.

1872　Published by Strahan.

1877　Published by Daldy, Isbister.

1882　Published by Routledge, New York.

1884　Published by Strahan.

[1886] Published by Blackie.

1900　Published by Blackie with the Hughes illustrations: cover design
　　　and frontispiece by Laurence Housman.

1909　Published by Lippincott, Philadelphia ('6th edition').

1911　Published by Blackie, pp.264, with the Hughes illustration.

1911　Published by Blackie, pp.viii, 391, with the Hughes illustrations+
　　　12 col. plates by Frank C. Papé.

1914　Published by Lippincott, Philadelphia: simplified by Elizabeth
　　　Lewis: illustrated.

1919　Published by McKay, Philadelphia: col. plates by Jessie Willcox
　　　Smith.

1924　Published by Macmillan, New York: with 13 illustrations by
　　　F. D. Bedford.

[n.d.] Published by Burt, New York: Dalton, New York: Lippincott,
　　　Philadelphia: McKay, Philadelphia.

[1926] Published by Blackie: illustrations by Hughes: col. frontispiece by
　　　Frank C. Papé: cover design by Laurence Housman.

1926　Published by McKay, Philadelphia: illustrated by Gertrude A.
　　　Kay.

1927 Published by Saalfield, New York: illustrated by Frances Brundage.

1934 Published by McKay, Philadelphia (reprint of 1926 edition).

[?1950] Published by Burt, New York: illustrated by George S. Graves.

1950 Published by Macmillan, New York: illustrated by George and Doris Hauman.

1956 Published by Garden City, New York: illustrated by Colleen Browning.

1956, with reprints to 1973 Published by J. M. Dent, London, and E. P. Dutton, New York; with 8 col. plates and line drawings by E. H. Shepard.

1958 Published by Collins; col. frontispiece and d/wrapper, and line drawings in text, by Will Nickless.

1960 Published by Gollancz, in *To the Land of Fair Delight: Three Victorian Tales of the Imagination*, with 19 of the Hughes illustrations. (The other two are 'Mopsa the Fairy', by Jean Ingelow, and 'The Little Panjandrum's Dodo', by G. E. Farrow.) Introduction (pp.5–8) by Noel Streatfeild.

1963 Published by Nonesuch, London. ⎤
1964 Published by F. Watts, New York. ⎦
'Nonesuch Cygnet' series, illustrated by Charles Mozley.

1964 Published by Macmillan, New York: illustrated by Harvey Dinnerstein: afterword by Clifton Fadiman.

1966 Published by University Microfilms, Ann Arbour, Michigan: facsimile, 'as originally published by Strahan in London in 1871 and by E. P. Dutton & Co., New York'.

1871

44. WORKS OF FANCY AND IMAGINATION. By George Mac-Donald, LL.D. Strahan & Co., 1871.

Ten vols: 16mo; green cloth, with design in gilt on front cover and spine, blind stamped on rear cover, all edges gilt; boxed, price 42*s*.

Vol.I: pp.viii, 345, (3): 'Within and Without' and 'A Hidden Life'.
Vol.II pp.viii, 288: Poems, including 'The Disciple'; 'The Gospel Women'; 'A Book of Sonnets'; and 'Organ Songs'.

| Vol. III | pp. viii, 288: Poems, comprising 'Violin Songs'; 'Songs of the Days and Nights'; 'A Book of Dreams'; 'Roadside Poems'; 'Poems for Children'. |

Vol. III   pp. viii, 288: Poems, comprising 'Violin Songs'; 'Songs of the Days and Nights'; 'A Book of Dreams'; 'Roadside Poems'; 'Poems for Children'.

Vol. IV: pp. viii, 304: Poems, comprising 'Parables', 'Ballads', and 'Scotch Songs and Ballads'.

Vol. V: pp. vi, 225, (1): 'Phantastes', part i.

Vol. VI: pp. vi, 217, (1): 'Phantastes', part ii.

Vol. VII: pp. viii, 278, (2): 'The Portent'.

Vol. VIII: pp. viii, 235, (1): 'The Light Princess'; 'The Giant's Heart'; 'The Shadows'.

Vol. IX: pp. viii, 270, (2): 'Cross Purposes'; 'The Golden Key'; 'The Carasoyn'; 'Little Daylight'.

Vol. X: pp. viii, 308: 'The Cruel Painter'; 'The Castle: a Parable'; 'The Wow o' Rivven'; 'The Broken Swords'; 'The Gray Wolf'; 'Uncle Cornelius His Story'.

'The Carasoyn' is here published for the first time in its complete form: the first 6 parts, entitled 'The Fairy Fleet: An English Märchen', appeared in *The Argosy*, April, 1866. The remainder appeared as 'The Fairy Cobbler', with a woodcut illustration by A. Houghton, in *Good Cheer*, December 25, 1867. 'Little Daylight' formed ch. 28 of *At the Back of the North Wind*, 1871.

1874   Reissued by Daldy, Isbister; green cloth.

1874   Reissued by Strahan.

1876   Reissued by Daldy.

1884   Reissued by Strahan, in 'grolier pattern' cloth.

1894   Reissued by Chatto & Windus, blue cloth, in a cloth case, 21*s.* the set. Also in 'grolier' cloth at 2*s.* 6*d.* per vol.

1905   Reissued by Chatto & Windus, as above.

1911   Chatto & Windus advertised 3 bindings: cloth with gilt top, 2*s.* per vol; 'grolier' cloth, 2*s.* 6*d.* per vol.; leather with gilt top, 3*s.* per vol. These were still being advertised in 1915.

1871

45. THE VICAR'S DAUGHTER: An Autobiographical Story. By George MacDonald. A sequel to *The Seaboard Parish* (1868), serialised in *The Sunday Magazine*, 1871–2, published by Alexander Strahan who also published the first edition in 1872. With 35 woodcut illustrations by F. A. Fraser.

1871

46. RANALD BANNERMAN'S BOYHOOD. By George Mac-
Donald. Strahan & Co., 1871.

8vo: pp.iv, 299, (1). Brick-red cloth, spine and front cover in gilt and
black, back cover blind-stamped, top edge gilt. With 24 page illustrations by Arthur Hughes, and 12 more in the text.

Serialised in *Good Words for the Young*, Nov., 1869–Oct., 1870. An
autobiographical story, many associations of which are traced in the *Life*.

1871　First American publication. Published by Routledge, New York.

1877　Published by Daldy.

1879　Published by Lippincott, Philadelphia.

1884　Published by Strahan.

1886　Published by Blackie, from the Strahan plates.

1889　Published by Lothrop, Boston.

n.d.　Published by Blackie.

n.d.　Published by Caldwell, Boston.

1900　Published by Blackie.

1911　Published by Blackie, pp.viii, 335, with 12 col. plates by A. V.
Wheelhouse and the 36 illustrations by Hughes.

1872

47. WILFRID CUMBERMEDE. By George MacDonald, LL.D.
Hurst & Blackett, 1872 [1871].

8vo: 3 vols: vol.I – pp.vi, 320; vol.II – pp.vi, 326, (2); vol.III – pp.vi, 291,
(1), (18 adv.). Blue cloth, covers stamped in black, spine in gilt and
black, plain edges.

With the subtitle 'An Autobiographical Story', this novel was serialised
in *St. Paul's*, Nov., 1870–Dec., 1871, and in *Scribner's Monthly*, Nov.,
1870–March, 1872 (q.v. 1870). It is partly set in Switzerland, where
MacDonald spent a summer holiday in 1865. Strahan paid MacDonald
£1,200 for the copyright (Bulloch, p.50).

Greville MacDonald (*Life*, p.351) believed that Ruskin's courtship of
Rose La Touche is reflected in the novel, and this view is interpreted in a
psychoanalytic vein by Wolff.

NELLY'S ESCAPE FROM THE KELPIE.

6. Illustration by Arthur Hughes to *Ranald Bannerman's Boyhood* (1871).

1872   First American publication. Published by Scribner, Armstrong, New York: 12mo, pp. viii, 498, with 11 plates.

1872   Published in 2 vols by Asher, Berlin (*Collection of English Authors*), pp. 305, 296.

1881   Published by Bedford, Clarke & Co., Chicago and St. Louis. Dark blue cloth, gilt front cover and spine.

1884   Published by Strahan ('4th edition').

1893   Published by Kegan Paul, pp. 528.

n.d.   Published by Kegan Paul, pp. 528.

1901   Published by Kegan Paul, price 1s. 6d.

[1911] Published by McKay, Philadelphia.

1872

48.   THE PRINCESS AND THE GOBLIN. By George MacDonald. Strahan & Co., 1872 [Dec., 1871]. With 30 illustrations by Arthur Hughes.

8vo: pp. vi, 313, (1). Green cloth: pictorial decorations, based on text illustrations by Hughes, on spine and front cover, in gilt and black. All edges gilt.

MacDonald referred to this story in a letter to his wife dated Feb. 25, 1871. '. . . I know it is as good work of the kind as I can do, and I think it will be the most complete thing I have done . . .' (*Life*, p. 412). It first appeared with the Hughes illustrations in *Good Words for the Young*, Nov., 1870–June, 1871.

1871   First American publication. Published by Routledge, New York.

[1880?] Published by Lippincott, Philadelphia.

1884   Published by Strahan.

1888 [1887]   Published by Blackie: pp. vi, 313, (1).

1889   Published by Lothrop, Boston.

[n.d.] Published by Blackie, pp. vi, 313, (1).

1899   Published by Burt, New York: 'Little Women' series.

1900 [1899]   Published by Blackie.

[19—] Published by Lippincott, Philadelphia.

"Perhaps. It will have more room by and by."

Curdie kept quite still. After a little while, hearing nothing but the sounds of their preparations for departure, mingled with an occa-

sional word of direction, and anxious to know whether the removal of the stone had made an opening into the goblins' house, he put in his hand to feel. It went in a good way, and then came in contact with something soft. He had but a moment to feel it over, it was so quickly withdrawn: it was one of the toeless goblin-feet. The owner of it gave a cry of fright.

"What's the matter, Helfer?" asked his mother.

"A beast came out of the wall and licked my foot."

"Nonsense! There are no wild beasts in our country," said his father.

"But it was, father. I felt it."

"Nonsense, I say. Will you malign your native realms and reduce them to a level with the country up stairs? That is swarming with wild beasts of every description."

"But I did feel it, father."

"I tell you to hold your tongue. You are no patriot."

Curdie suppressed his laughter, and lay still as a mouse—but no stiller, for every moment he kept nibbling away with his fingers at the edges of the hole. He was slowly making it bigger, for here the rock had been very much shattered with the blasting.

There seemed to be a good many in the

family, to judge from the mass of confused talk which now and then came through the hole; but when all were speaking together, and just as if they had bottle-brushes—each at least one—in their throats, it was not easy to make out much that was said. At length he heard once more what the father-goblin was saying.

"Now then," he said, "get your bundles on your backs. Here, Helfer, I'll help you up with your chest."

"I wish it *was* my chest, father."

"Your turn will come in good time enough! Make haste. I *must* go to the meeting at the palace to-night. When that's over, we can come back and clear out the last of the things before our enemies return in the morning. Now light your torches, and come along. What a distinction it is to provide our own light, instead of being dependent on a thing hung up in the air—a most disagreeable contrivance—intended no doubt to blind us when we venture out under its baleful influence! Quite glaring and vulgar, I call it, though no doubt useful to poor creatures who haven't the wit to make light for themselves!"

Curdie could hardly keep himself from calling through to know whether they made

the fire to light their torches by. But a moment's reflection showed him that they would have said they did, inasmuch as they struck two stones together, and the fire came.

7. First appearance of *The Princess and Goblin* in *Good Words for the Young* (1871) with illustrations by Arthur Hughes.

1907   Published by Lippincott, Philadelphia, with the Hughes illustrations plus col. plates by Maria L. Kirk.

1907   Published by Caldwell, Boston.

1911   Published by Blackie: pp.308, with the Hughes illustrations plus 12 col. plates by Helen Stratton.

[n.d.]   Published by Blackie, as above.

1913   Published by Lippincott, Philadelphia: simplified by Elizabeth Lewis: 12mo, pp.124, with col. plates by Maria L. Kirk: in the series *George MacDonald Stories for Little Folk.*

1920   Published by McKay, Philadelphia; 8vo, pp.203, with col. illustrations by Jessie Wilcox Smith.

1926   Published by Macmillan, New York, with illustrations by F. D. Bedford.

1927   Published by Saalfield, New York, with illustrations by Frances Brundage.

1928, 1937   Published by Doubleday, Doran, New York, with illustrations by Elizabeth MacKinstry; pp.viii, 271.

[1934?]   Published by Lippincott, Philadelphia, with the Hughes' illustrations and col. plates by Maria L. Kirk.

[1934]   Published by McKay, Philadelphia; pp.263, with col. plates by Jessie Wilcox Smith.

[1937]   Published by Garden City, New York, with illustrations by Elizabeth MacKinstry.

1948   Published by Watergate Classics Ltd, with illustrations by Arthur Hughes, in the *Watergate Children's Classics,* edited by John Betjeman: pp.vi, 163.

1949, with reprints to 1973   Published by Dent, London, and Dutton, New York with 8 col. plates by Charles Folkard.

[1951]   Published by Macmillan, New York, with illustrations by Nora S. Unwin.

[1955]   Published by Exposition Press, New York; adapted for reading in the middle grades by Margaret Tommasini.

[1956]   Published by Collins, with illustrations by Will Nickless.

1957   Abridged edition, published by Collins, Glasgow: pp.96.

[1959]   Published by Random House, New York, with the Hughes' illustrations.

[1960] Published by Blackie: illustrations by Jane Paton, pp.239.

1964, with reprints to 1973   Published by Penguin Books; with the Hughes' illustrations.

1967   Published by University Microfilms, Ann Arbour, Michigan: facsimile, pp.249.

1967   Published by Airmont, New York, with the Hughes' illustrations and cover design by Jules Gotlieb: introduction by Alice H. Hogan.

1970   *The Princess and the Goblin & The Princess and Curdie*: abridged by Olive Jones. Published by American Education Publications, Middletown, Conn. Illustrations (part col.) by William Stobbs.

1970   *The Princess and the Goblin & The Princess and Curdie*: abridged. Published by Collins.

1971   Braille edition, 2 vols: published by the Royal National Institute for the Blind.

1973   Published by Blackie; illustrated.

1872

49.   THE VICAR'S DAUGHTER: an Autobiographical Story. By George MacDonald, LL.D. Tinsley Brothers, 1872.

8vo: 3 vols: vol.I – pp.vi, 290; vol.II – pp.vi, 289, (1); vol. III – pp.viii [i and ii advertise works by MacDonald], 325, (1), [327 and 328 advertise works by MacDonald]. Dark-green cloth, two gilt ornaments on each cover, connected with gilt bands across spine, the design uniform with that of *The Seaboard Parish*, 1868. Plain edges. Serialised in *The Sunday Magazine*, 1871–2.

A sequel to *The Seaboard Parish*, set in London and Hastings. A review in the *Athenaeum*, Aug. 10, 1872, described the parables as 'dark and unintelligible'. The publisher was Alexander Strahan, who paid MacDonald £1,000 for the story (Bulloch, p. 48): Strahan appears in the 'Introductory' as 'Mr. S' who 'is not like any other publisher . . . for he is so fond of good work that he never grumbles at any alterations writers choose to make' – a reference to MacDonald's addiction to extensive revision. He implies that Strahan pressed him to write the story 'to complete the *trilogy*, as he called it' (p.4), the first two parts being *Annals of a Quiet Neighbourhood* (1867) and *The Seaboard Parish* (1868), which are mentioned by name on p.3. 'I have a weakness in the direction of the sensible,' says Mr. S (pp.17, 18), which is consistent with Strahan's views that *Good Words for the Young* had, at one time, 'too much of the fairy element' (q.v., 1868). 'Lady Bernard' is a life-like portrait of Lady Byron (d.1860).

In a letter to his wife from Huntly, dated May 20, 1872, MacDonald wrote:

> 'I must try to work on my proofs in the trains, or I don't know how I shall get through with the last of the *Vicar* which is now being lugged from me' (*Life*, p.418).

1871 First American publication. Published by Robert Bros., Boston, with 6 plates.

1872 Published by Tauchnitz, Leipzig, in 2 vols. (*Collection of British Authors*).

1879 Published by Munro, New York ('Seaside Library').

1881 Published by Sampson Low.

[189?] Published by Routledge, New York: illustrated.

1893 Published with a frontispiece heliogravure of Elliott & Fry's portrait by Lemercier, Paris.

1902 Published by R. E. King, price 6*d*.

1905 Published by Newnes.

1908 Published by Edwin Dalton from the Newnes plates.

[1911] Published by McKay, Philadelphia.

1873

50. SPIRITUAL SONGS [of Novalis]. Pp.[8], paper wrappers. Privately printed by Innes, Hammersmith.

This is the second version of *Twelve of the Spiritual Songs of Novalis*, 1851, with three additional songs. The front cover has a note about Novalis, and states: 'I offer this, like a sheet of Christmas carols, to my friend.' It is signed 'Christmas, 1873, George MacDonald'. The caption title, 'Spiritual Songs', is on p.[3]. There are two copies in the Houghton Library, Harvard, one inscribed to MacDonald's daughter Irene, the other to MacDonald's literary agent, A. P. Watt. These translations were incorporated into *Exotics*, 1876, and *Rampolli*, 1897.

1873

51.   GUTTA PERCHA WILLIE, THE WORKING GENIUS. By George MacDonald. Henry S. King, 1873.

8vo: pp.iv, 212, (28 adv., dated Jan., 1873).

Blue cloth, spine and front cover in gilt and black, rear cover in black, top edge gilt, design featuring Willie and the baby on front cover. Price 3s. 6d. 'Reprinted from "Good Words for the Young"' (p.iv). Frontispiece plus 8 page illustrations by Arthur Hughes. The illustration of Willie and Mrs. Wilson facing p.10 lacks Hughes' monogram, and is signed 'F A' in the bottom right corner. Serialised, with the above illustrations, as *The History of Gutta Percha Willie*, in *Good Words for the Young*, 1873 (q.v., 1868).

1873   First American publication. Published by Hoyt, Boston.

1874   Published by Henry S. King: 'Second Edition'.

[1887] Published by Blackie as *The History of Gutta Percha Willie*, with 8 of the illustrations by Hughes.

1900   Published by Scribner, New York.

1901   Published by Blackie.

1903   Published by Union Press, Philadelphia.

1917   Published by Hodder and Stoughton.

[n.d.] Published by the American Sunday School Union, Philadelphia.

1875

52.   MALCOLM. By George MacDonald. [Motto] 'The greatest step is that out of doors' [Jacula Prudentum of George Herbert]. Henry S. King & Co., 1875 [1874].

8vo: 3 vols: vol.I – pp.viii, 286, (32 adv. dated Sept., 1874); vol.II – pp.viii, 317, (1); vol.III – pp.viii, 355, (1). Apple-green cloth, gilt spine, uncut edges.

The 'Portlossie' of this novel, and of its sequel, 'The Marquis of Lossie' (1877) is Cullen, Banffshire, where MacDonald spent several summers gathering material. The blind piper was drawn from a certain Farquhar Gillanders, so Greville MacDonald was informed, though the idea was based on the escape from Culloden of George MacDonald's great-grandfather, William MacDonald (*Life*, pp.40, 41, 466).

Mr. Hugh L. Cheyne, then living at 26 Grant Street, Cullen, where

Malcolm was said to have been written, related that when the story was serialised in the *Glasgow Herald*, there was a perfect rush for the paper, the purchasers asking not for the *Herald*, but simply for 'Makim' (Bulloch, p.29).

1875 First American publication. Published by Lippincott, Philadelphia.

1876 Published by Henry S. King ('Second edition', in 3 vols).

1876 Published by Tauchnitz, Leipzig, in 2 vols ('Collection of British Authors'), pp.325, 318.

1877 Published by Kegan Paul ('Third edition'), pp.viii, 438, with steel-engraved portrait.

1877 Published by Lippincott, Philadelphia.

1879 Published by Kegan Paul ('Fourth edition').

1880 Published by Munro, New York ('Seaside Library').

1883 Published by Kegan Paul ('Sixth edition').

[1884] Published by Kegan Paul ('Seventh edition').

n.d. Published by Kegan Paul ('Indian and Colonial Series').

[189?] Published by Routledge, New York.

1891 Published by Kegan Paul.

[1892] Published by Kegan Paul ('New edition').

1900 Published by Kegan Paul, price 1s. 6d.

1901 Published by Newnes, price 6d.

[1911] Published by McKay, Philadelphia.

1913 Published in 'Everett's Library'.

1927 Published by Cassell, pp.viii, 438.

1875

53. ST. GEORGE AND ST. MICHAEL. Serialised in the *Graphic*, April 24, 1875–Oct. 16, 1875, with 25 illustrations by Sydney P. Hall. Published in book form in 1875 (dated 1876, q.v.).

1875

54.   THE WISE WOMAN, A PARABLE. By George MacDonald. Strahan & Co., 1875.

8vo: pp.iv, 222, (2). Blue or grey cloth, lettering and decoration on front cover in gilt and black; gilt spine. Strahan's anchor device in gilt on front cover and spine. Plain edges.

Serialised under the title 'A Double Story' in *Good Things*, Dec. 5, 1874 to July 3, 1875 (see under *Good Words for the Young, etc*, 1868). Reviewed in the *Athenaeum*, Jan. 29, 1876. Though sub-titled 'a parable', it is in fact a fairy story, and has been reprinted under various titles, given below.

1876   First American publication. Published in the USA as *A Double Story* by Dodd, Mead, New York, and by Lothrop, Boston.

[1879] Published as *Princess Rosamond, a Double Story*, by Lothrop, Boston.

[1883] Published by Cassell from the Strahan plates, pp.222, '4th edition', price 3*s. 6d*.

[1884] Published as *A Double Story* by Lothrop, Boston.

1886   Published by Cassell, price 2*s. 6d*.

1895   Published as *The Lost Princess; or The Wise Woman*, by Wells, Gardner, Darton & Co. 8vo, pp.x, 258, blue cloth, with 22 illustrations by A. G. Walker.

[n.d.] As above, in red cloth.

1965   Published as *The Lost Princess: a Double Story*, by Dent (London) and Dutton (New York), with 4 col. plates and line drawings by D. J. Watkins-Pitchford.

1972   Included as 'The Wise Woman' by Pan/Ballantine (paperback), in a collection of 3 stories by MacDonald, in their 'Adult Fantasy' series edited by Lin Carter, under the general title *Evenor*. The other stories in this volume are 'The Carasoyn' and 'The Golden Key'. 'The Wise Woman' occupies pp.3–115, and has a separate preface (p.2), in which the story is described as 'too deep and powerful for the young', and 'a strange and baffling book'. (See also *Evenor*, 1972, under *Dealings with the Fairies*, 1867).

1973   Included as *The Wise Woman or The Lost Princess: A Double Story* in vol.I of the Eerdmans/Mowbray collection (see under *The Gifts of the Child Christ*, 1882).

1876

55. ST. GEORGE AND ST. MICHAEL. By George MacDonald. Henry S. King, 1876 [1875].

8vo: 3 vols: vol.I – pp.vi, 249, (3), (47 adv. dated Oct., 1875); vol.II – pp.vi, 312; vol.III – pp.viii, 306, (2). Brown cloth, gilt spine, covers with blind-stamped borders, plain edges.

Serialised in the *Graphic*, April 24, 1875–Oct. 16, 1875. This story of Royalists and Puritans was so called because the heroine and hero were born on St. George's Day and St. Michael's Day. It was the only historical novel written by MacDonald. The interest centres on Raglan Castle and the Marquis of Worcester. Vol.III ends with a note:

> 'Whoever cares to distinguish the bones of fact from the drapery of invention in the foregone tale, will find them all in the late Dr. Dirick's "Life of the Marquis of Worcester", and the "Certamen Religiosum" and "Golden Apophthegms" of Dr. Bayly.'

[1876?] First American publication. Published by J. B. Ford, New York: 12mo, pp.vi, 552, with 7 plates and a portrait ('Author's Edition').

1876 Published by Tauchnitz, Leipzig, in 2 vols, pp.311, 294 ('Collection of British Authors').

1878 Published by Kegan Paul, with frontispiece ('second edition').

1880 Published by Munro, New York ('Seaside Library').

1883 Published by Kegan Paul ('third edition').

[1884] Published by Kegan Paul ('fourth edition').

1892 Published by Kegan Paul.

[189?] Published by Routledge, New York.

1899 Published by Kegan Paul.

1900 Published by Kegan Paul.

1910 Published by Hodder & Stoughton, price 6*d*.

[1911] Published by McKay, Philadelphia.

1876

56. THOMAS WINGFOLD, CURATE. Serialised in *Day of Rest* (weekly, Jan.–Dec., 1876). Published in book form in Dec., 1876 (q.v.).

57. THE ELDER HAMLET. *Macmillan's Magazine*, August, 1876. Reprinted in *Orts*, 1882 and *A Dish of Orts*, 1883.

58. THE MARQUIS OF LOSSIE. A sequel to *Malcolm* (1875), serialised in *Lippincott's Magazine* (USA), Nov., 1876–Sept., 1877, and in the *Glasgow Weekly Mail* (Bulloch, p.29). Published in book form in 1877 (q.v.).

1876

59. THOMAS WINGFOLD, CURATE. By George MacDonald, LL.D. Hurst & Blackett, [Dec.] 1876.

8vo: 3 vols: vol.I – pp.iv, 294; vol.II – pp.iv, 314; vol.III – pp.305, (3), (16 adv.). Light-blue cloth, ornamental front cover stamped in black, spine gilt and black, plain edges.

Serialised in *Day of Rest*, Jan.–Dec., 1876. This novel deals with a young clergyman who, entering the church simply as a profession, attains true faith. Andrew Lang, in the *Fortnightly Review* (Jan., 1877), declared the book likely to encourage 'unhealthy feeling'. Wingfold reappears in *Paul Faber, Surgeon* (1879), and *There and Back* (1891).

1876   First American publication. Published by Routledge, New York.

1879   Published by Munro, New York ('Seaside Library').

[1880] Published by Strahan.

1883   Published by Chatto & Windus: frontispiece by C. J. Staniland.

1886   Published by Kegan Paul.

1893   Published by Kegan Paul.

1901   Published by Kegan Paul.

[1911] Published by McKay, Philadelphia.

1876

60. EXOTICS. A Translation of the Spiritual Songs of Novalis, the Hymn-Book of Luther, and other Poems from the German and Italian. By George MacDonald, Strahan & Co. 1876.

8vo: pp.xvi, [192]. Some pages preceding p.177, and all the remaining pages, are not numbered. The British Library Catalogue gives the pagination as 177. Cloth: olive green or light brown or light cobalt blue. Gilt lettering and floral decoration on spine and front cover. All edges plain. The design on the front cover is of a clump of cyclamen and a hand holding a trowel, within a rectangular border. The choice of this design is explained in the preface (p.ix):

'In the flower-pots of translation, to vary the figure on my title page, I offer you these few exotics . . .'

However, the design does not appear on the title page.
Contents, pp.[v]–vii.
[Preface, headed] *To My Friends*, pp.[ix]–xv.
The Spiritual Songs of Novalis (I–XV), pp.[3]–[36].
Luther's Song Book, pp.[37]–116.
From Schiller, (11 poems), pp.[117]–134.
From Goethe, (3 poems), pp.[135]–143.
From Uhland, (2 poems), pp.[145–150].
From Heine, (4 poems), pp.[151]–165.
From Von Salis-Seewis, (2 poems), pp.[167]–172.
From Claudius, (2 poems), pp.[173]–177.
From Milton, (6 Italian poems), pp.[179–186].
From Petrarch, (2 sonnets), pp.[187–190].
Song of the Lonely, from the German, p.[191].
Three Pairs and One: a trans-translation from the German poet Ruckert, through the Dutch poet Genestet, p.[192].

The preface sets out the author's principles of translation, and is a revised reprint of the preface to the translation of Luther's Hymn Book 'when that was first uttered some years ago in a periodical'. MacDonald gives no clue as to the identity or date of the periodical: it was, in fact, *The Sunday Magazine*, 1866–7 (q.v.). These principles, six in number, are expounded in conversational form, the first and most important being that 'the spirit of the writer must be given.' It is admitted that 'a perfect translation from one language into another is an absolute impossibility'. MacDonald also remarks that he bestowed on the Spiritual Songs of Novalis 'twice the labour spent upon all the rest of the book together'. *Exotics* is thus the first collected edition of MacDonald's translations, later extended in *Rampolli*, 1897.

1877

61.   THE MARQUIS OF LOSSIE. By George MacDonald, LL.D. Hurst & Blackett, 1877.

8v: 3 vols: vol.I – pp.iv, 320; vol.II – pp.iv, 309, (1); vol.III – pp.iv, 307, (3), (16 adv.). Olive-green cloth, spine in gilt and black, covers blind-stamped, lettering on front cover in black, plain edges.

Serialised in *Lippincott's Magazine* (USA), Nov., 1876–Sept., 1877, and in the *Glasgow Weekly Mail* (Bulloch, p.29), this novel is a sequel to *Malcolm* (1875). There is a reference, in ch.14, to the parable from *The Disciples at Sais* by Novalis, which MacDonald translated and published in *Rampolli* (1897).

1877   First American publication. Published by Lippincott, Philadelphia, pp.245.

1877   Published by Fergus, Chicago ('Popular Library').

1877   Published by Tauchnitz, Leipzig, in 2 vols. ('Collection of British Authors').

1878   Published by Kegan Paul; pp.viii, 386, with woodcut frontispiece.

1879   Published by Kegan Paul; as above, '3rd edition'.

1881   Published by Munro, New York ('Seaside Library').

1883   Published by Kegan Paul; '4th edition', with frontispiece.

[1884] Published by Kegan Paul; '5th edition', with frontispiece.

[1886] Published by Lothrop, Boston.

1892   Published by Kegan Paul.

[189?] Published by Burt, New York, and Routledge, New York.

1900   Published by Kegan Paul.

[1900 or 1901]   Published by Newnes, in double columns, price 6*d*.

[1911] Published by McKay, Philadelphia.

1913   Published in Everett's Library.

1927   Published by Cassell, pp.viii, 386.

1878

62.   A LETTER TO AMERICAN BOYS. This letter of approx. 3,000 words, beginning 'My Dear Cousins' and ending 'Your friend George MacDonald', was published in the USA.

It consists mostly of a parable: the first part describes the author's room in 'The Retreat' overlooking the River Thames, where the letter was written. It is reprinted in the Eerdmans/Mowbray collection, *The Gifts of the Child Christ*, 1973 (q.v. 1882), where it occupies pp.10–16 of the introduction.

1879

63.   PAUL FABER, SURGEON. By George MacDonald, LL.D.
Hurst & Blackett, 1879 [Dec., 1878].

8vo: 3 vols: vol.I – pp.vi, 300; vol.II – pp.iv, 309, (1); vol.III – pp.iv, 283, (3), (16 adv.). Light-brown cloth, spine in gilt and black, front cover stamped in black, rear cover blind-stamped, plain edges.

Dedication: 'Tuum est' – one 8-line stanza, to W.C[owper]. T[emple], signed 'G.M.D, Forto Fino, Dec. 1878'.

A sequel to *Thomas Wingfold, Curate* (1876). Strahan declined to serialise this novel in his newly-launched *Day of Rest*, but bought the rights for a 3-volume first edition for £400 – less than half of what MacDonald had recently been getting for his novels. According to Greville MacDonald, his father thought *Paul Faber* the best of his novels (*Life*, p.353). The greater part of ch.6, vol.II, 'The Groans of the Inarticulate', was published separately as a pamphlet by the Illinois Anti-Vivisectionist Society [189?] – it was probably based on a sermon preached at Arundel. Ronald MacDonald points out further associations with Arundel in *From a Northern Window* (1911).

1879   First American publication. Published by Lippincott, Philadelphia, pp.201.

1879   Published by Munro, New York ('Seaside Library').

1881   Published by Strahan.

1883   Published by Chatto & Windus, with frontispiece by J. E. Millais.

1886   Published by Kegan Paul.

1893   Published by Kegan Paul.

n.d.   Published by Kegan Paul ('6th edition').

1901   Published by Kegan Paul ('7th edition').

[1911] Published by McKay, Philadelphia.

1879

64.   SIR GIBBIE. By George MacDonald, LL.D. Hurst & Blackett, 1879.

8vo, 3 vols: vol.I – pp.iv, 320; vol.II – p.iv, 316; vol.III – pp.iv, 318, (2), (16 adv.). Olive-brown cloth, gilt spine, plain edges.

'This story, which was written at Porto Fino, was serialised in the *Glasgow Weekly Mail* (vol.iii), Jan. 4–March 15, 1879 (file in Mitchell

Library, Glasgow). Sir Edward Troup thinks it was also serialised in New Zealand. Dr Greville MacDonald says (*Life*, p.488) it was serialised in *Lippincott's Magazine*, but this is not so (Bulloch, p.43). In a letter dated June 19, 1878, MacDonald noted that 'a new story' ['Sir Gibbie'] was 'more than half done' (*Life*, p.487). The book was reviewed in the *British Quarterly Review*, Oct., 1879, and *The Athenaeum*, June 14, 1879.

The central character, the dumb urchin Gibbie, in reality Sir Gilbert Galbraith, is one of the most original of MacDonald's creations. Greville MacDonald, in his introduction to the 'Everyman' edition of 1914, wrote:

'*Sir Gibbie* is, I think, at once the most direct and the most beautiful of all George MacDonald's novels. . . . His life's warfare against vulgarity in art, professionalism in religion, wage estimate of labour, dogmatic interpretations of the Infinite Love, class-worship and spiritual wickedness in high places, marches through the pages of this book with bagpipes and bonnet and broadsword. . . .'

1879   First American publication. 'Author's edition by Lippincott, Philadelphia: 8vo, pp.210 (New York Pub. Lib.)' (Bulloch, p.44).

1879   Published in Munro's Seaside Library, New York.

1880   Published by Hurst & Blackett in one vol., pp.iv, 390, with a frontispiece by E. Hughes.

[n.d.] Published by Hurst & Blackett, as above.

1880   Published by Tauchnitz, Leipzig, in 2 vols, in their *Collection of British Authors*, pp.320 and 304.

[190?] Published by Burt, New York.

1900   Published by Hurst & Blackett, pp.390, price 3*s.* 6*d.*

1906   Published by Hurst & Blackett, price 6*d.*

1911   Published by McKay, Philadelphia.

1914   Published by J. M. Dent, London, and E. P. Dutton, New York, in the 'Everyman Library'. Pp.xii, 436, with an introduction by Greville MacDonald (pp.vii–ix), and a short bibliography. Reprinted 1929.

1927   Published by Cassell, pp.vii, 390.

1963 ⎱ Published by ⎱ Dutton, New York, pp.270.
1967 ⎰   ⎰ Blackie, pp.xvii, 249.
        Abridged edition, edited and with a foreword by Elizabeth Yates: '. . . I have cut the original *Sir Gibbie* almost by half, taking out the pages that were a digression from the story; and I have 'translated'

the Scotch dialect into English, except for certain flavourful words which have long been familiar.' The chapters have been reduced from 62 to 22. There is a short glossary of Scottish words.

1879

65. THE HISTORY OF PHOTOGEN AND NYCTERIS: A DAY AND NIGHT MÄRCHEN. This fairy tale (sometimes reprinted as *The Day Boy and the Night Girl*) first appeared in the Christmas number of *The Graphic*, 1879. For reprints, see under *Dealings with the Fairies*, 1867, and *The Gifts of the Child Christ*, 1882.

1880

66. A BOOK OF STRIFE IN THE FORM OF 'THE DIARY OF AN OLD SOUL'. By George MacDonald. Printed for the Author, and to be had by writing to Mr. Hughes, 43 Beaufort Street, Chelsea, London. 1880. Price Five Shillings.

8vo: pp.268, of which the last 3 are blank except for the imprint of Unwin Brothers, Printers. Bound in red cloth, with printed label on spine.

This book is unique among the first editions of MacDonald in its proportions (cover: cm: 16.8×8) and in being printed on one side of the leaf only, though pagination is continuous. The purpose is explained in the dedication, signed 'Your Old Soul':

> 'Sweet friends, receive my offering. You will find
> Against each worded page a white page set:–
> This is the mirror of each friendly mind
> Reflecting that. In this book we are met.
> Make it, dear hearts, of worth to you indeed:–
> Let your white page be ground, my print to seed,
> Growing to golden ears, that faith and hope shall feed.'

The *Diary* is a poem of 366 7-line stanzas (not 365 as stated in the *Life*, p.496, and in Bulloch, p.13), one for each day of the year, numbered as days of the month. The opening of the stanza for February 29 is characteristic of MacDonald's fusion of the factual and the metaphorical:

> 'Gather my broken fragments to a whole,
> As these four quarters make a shining day.'

A BOOK OF STRIFE

IN THE FORM OF

The Diary of an Old Soul

BY

GEORGE MAC DONALD

*Printed for the Author, and to be had by
writing to*

MR. HUGHES, 43, BEAUFORT STREET, CHELSEA,
LONDON.

—

1880.

Price Five Shillings.

8. Title page of the first edition of *The Book of Strife* (1880).

Go not forth to call thy sorrow
From the dim fields of tomorrow;
Let her roam there all unheeded;
She will come when she is needed;
But when she draws nigh thy door,
She will find God there before.

DEDICATION

Sweet friends, receive my offering. You will find
Against each worded page a white page set :—
This is the mirror of each friendly mind
Reflecting that. In this book we are met.
Make it, dear hearts, of worth to you indeed :—
Let your white page be ground, my print be seed,
Growing to golden ears, that faith and hope shall feed.

YOUR OLD SOUL

George MacDonald.

9. Original poem by GMD in manuscript signed by the author,
apparently not reproduced elsewhere, appearing on the dedication
page of a later edition of *The Book of Strife* (1889).

The *Life* (p.497) quotes a correspondent who heard Ruskin praise the *Diary* in an Oxford lecture. 'Everybody is asking today what that 'Diary' is. Nobody seems to have heard of it until Mr Ruskin mentioned it. I believe it has not been advertised, indeed is sold almost privately.' Ruskin described it as 'one of the three great sacred poems of the nineteenth century'.

When a new edition was being considered, MacDonald, in a letter to his friend and literary agent A. P. Watt dated Nov. 7, 1884, asked that no copies be distributed for review (ibid.). Presumably this refers to Longmans' edition of 1885, given by Bulloch.

1885   Published by Longmans: price 12*s*. 6*d*. 'It never had any sale in this form and Dr Greville MacDonald bought all their rights, and has found the sale steadily growing' (Bulloch, p.13).

1889   Published Longmans and Green, London and New York.

[*c*.1890]   Published by Longmans: 18mo, price 6*s*.

1902   Published by Longmans: 12mo, price 6*s*.

1905   Published as *The Diary of an Old Soul and translations of other spiritual verse*, by Arthur C. Fifield: this is a reprint of *Rampolli*, 1897 (q.v.).

1905   (December). Published by Fifield, pp.170, with a portrait as frontispiece.

1905   Published by J. M. Dent from the Fifield plates, with a portrait as frontispiece. Reprinted 1906, 1909, 1913, 1922.

1924   Published by George Allen & Unwin, with a portrait. Reprinted 1927.

1881

67.   MARY MARSTON. By George MacDonald, LL.D. Sampson Low, Marston, Searle, & Rivington, 1881.

8vo: vol.I – pp.viii, 336; vol.II – pp.iv, 338, (2); vol.III – pp.iv, 324, (32 adv. dated April, 1880). Black cloth, gilt spine, covers blind-stamped, plain edges.

Dedication (p.v), in one four-line stanza, to William J. Matheson, signed 'G.M.D., Casa Coraggio, Bordighera'.

The setting of this novel is a draper's shop.

1881   'Fifth Edition', by Sampson Low, pp.viii, 355, (1).

1881   First American publication. Published by Appleton, New York.

1881 'Authorised Edition', by Lippincott, Philadelphia.

1881 Published in Munro's Seaside Library, New York.

1881 Published by Tauchnitz, Leipzig, in 2 vols.

1894 Published by Sampson, Low.

1905 Published by Newnes.

1908 Published by Edwin Dalton, pp.viii, 355, with illustrations by Cyrus Cuneo and G. H. Evison.

1881

68. WARLOCK O'GLEN WARLOCK: Serialised in monthly supplements to *Wide Awake* (USA: ? published by Lothrop, Boston). Published in book form by Lothrop, Boston, in September or October, 1881.

68A. WARLOCK O'GLEN WARLOCK: A Homely Romance. Lothrop, Boston (n.d., 'Copyright 1881, D Lothrop & Co' on verso of title leaf).

8vo, pp.(2) + 741+4 ad. Olive-green cloth, gilt spine, red-brown horizontal decoration on front cover and spine, plain edges. Price 1$75.

Bullock gives a facsimile of the contract between the author and Sampson Low, Marston, Searle, and Rivington dated March, 1881; publication date is given as 'on or about September 15, 1881' and the title as *Warlock of Glen Warlock*. No less than 3 editions were published in the USA in 1881 – by Lothrop, Boston; Lee and Shepard, Boston; and Harpers, New York ('Franklin Square Library'). The Lothrop edition, described above, has been seen by the compiler: it is inscribed October 29, 1881 and, together with evidence of copyright date, can be accepted as the true first edition. The publisher's ad states:

'The present story, which is printed from the author's manuscript, was orginally published in monthly parts, as supplements to *Wide Awake.*'

Later editions are given under *Castle Warlock*, 1882 (q.v.).

1882

69.   CASTLE WARLOCK: A Homely Romance. Sampson Low, Marston, Searle, and Rivington, 1882.

8vo: 3 vols: vol.I – pp.iv+334+(2); vol.II – pp.iv+309+(1)+32 ads dated Dec., 1881; vol.III – pp.iv+374+(2). Brown cloth, spine in gilt and black, covers with black borders, plain edges. Dedicated to Mrs Russell Gurney, to whom MacDonald had been introduced by Lady Byron, in three 4-line stanzas dated Bordighera, March, 1882.

This is the second (first English) edition; it was first published by Lothrop, Boston, in 1881 as *Warlock O'Glen Warlock*.

1882   Published by Munro, New York ('Seaside Library').

1883   Published by Kegan Paul, 'Second Edition' with frontispiece by H.M.P(aget).

(n.d.)   Published by Engelmann, Berlin ('Ascher's Collection of English Authors') 3 vols.

1885   Published by Lothrop, Boston, as *Warlock O'Glen Warlock*, illustrated.

1890   Published by Kegan Paul, 'Fourth Edition'.

(1892) Published by Kegan Paul.

(1900) Published by Kegan Paul.

1882

70.   WEIGHED AND WANTING. Serialised in *The Sunday Magazine*, Jan.–Dec., 1882. Published in book form late in 1882.

1882

71.   THE GIFTS OF THE CHILD CHRIST, AND OTHER TALES. By George MacDonald. Sampson Low, Marston, Searle, & Rivington, 1882.

8vo: 2 vols: vol.I – pp.iv, 283, (1): vol.II – pp.iv, 268, (32 adv. dated Dec., 1881). Olive green cloth; device embodying publishers' initials blind-stamped on covers; gilt spine; plain edges.

Contents: Vol.I – (i) The Gifts of the Child Christ; (ii) The History of Photogen and Nycteris, a Day and Night Märchen; (iii) The Butcher's Bills. Vol.II – (iv) Stephen Archer; (v) Port in a Storm; (vi) If I had a Father [a drama in 4 acts].

'The History of Photogen and Nycteris' first appeared in the Christmas number of *The Graphic*, 1879. It has often been reprinted with Mac-Donald's other fairy tales (see *Dealings with the Fairies*, 1867).

'Port in a Storm' first appeared in *The Argosy*, Nov., 1866. The other items in this collection are new.

'If I had a Father' was written almost a quarter of a century earlier, and formed the basis of an unpublished novel, *Seekers and Finders* [?1860, q.v.]. It was severely criticised in the *Athenaeum* review of April 29, 1882, and seems never to have been performed.

1882 Published by Tauchnitz, Leipzig, in one vol.

1883 First American publication. Published in Munro's Seaside Library, New York, omitting 'Stephen Archer' and 'Port in a Storm'.

1883 *Stephen Archer and Other Tales*; published by Sampson Low, pp.vi, 354. This volume is as the first edition, except for the change of title and the placing of the fourth item, 'Stephen Archer', in front. Reprinted 1894.

[n.d.] *Stephen Archer*; published by McKay, Philadelphia.

1905 *Stephen Archer*; published by Newnes: pp.360.

1908 *Stephen Archer*; published from the Newnes plates by Edwin Dalton.

1971 *Stephen Archer*; published by Books for Libraries Press, Freeport, New York. A reprint of *Stephen Archer and Other Tales*, as published by Sampson Low, 1883.

1973 *The Gifts of the Child Christ: Fairytales and Stories for the Childlike.* Edited by Glenn Edward Sadler. Published by William B. Eerdmans Publishing Co., Grand Rapids, Michigan, and by A. R. Mowbray & Co., Oxford. 8vo: 2 vols: vol.I – pp.333, (3): vol.II – pp.261, (3). (The Mowbray edition was issued in March, 1974, in hardback, boxed.) Printed in the USA.

Contents: vol.I – Coloured frontispiece of MacDonald, from chromolithograph in the British Musueum: prefatory note from a grand-daughter of MacDonald, dated May 7, 1972 (p.5): intro-duction by Glenn Edward Sadler (pp.9–21): 'The Fantastic Im-agination' (reprinted from *A Dish of Orts*, 1893, and originally published as the preface to *The Light Princess and other fairy tales*, G. P. Putnam's Sons, New York, [1893]: see under *Dealings with the Fairies*, 1867): and the following stories, with first appearances in brackets:

(1) 'The Gifts of the Child Christ'. (*The Gifts of the Child Christ and Other Tales*, 1882.)

(2) 'The History of Photogen and Nycteris'. (As above.)

(3) 'The Shadows'. (*Adela Cathcart*, 1864.)

(4) 'Little Daylight'. (June, 1870, in *Good Words for the Young*, as part of *At the Back of the North Wind*, not in *Works of Fancy and Imagination*, 1871, as given on p.135, nor did the Hughes illustration on p.134 appear in the latter, as stated.)

(5) 'The Golden Key'. (*Dealings with the Fairies*, 1867.)

(6) 'Cross Purposes'. (*Dealings with the Fairies*, 1867.)

(7) 'The Wise Woman, or The Lost Princess: A Double Story'. (Serialised as 'A Double Story', in *Good Things*, Dec., 1874–July, 1875.)

(8) 'The Castle: A Parable'. (*Adela Cathcart*, 1864.)

(9) 'Port in a Storm'. (*Argosy*, Nov., 1866.)

(10) 'Papa's Story [A Scot's (sic) Christmas Story]'. (*Illustrated London News*, Dec. 23, 1865.)

Vol.II – Frontispiece: the MacDonald family, *c*.1872. 'The Girl That Lost Things': a poem by MacDonald.

(1) 'The Light Princess'. (*Adela Cathcart*, 1864.)

(2) 'The Giant's Heart'. (Published as 'Tell Us A Story', in the Christmas number of *Illustrated London News*, Dec., 19, 1863.)

(3) 'The Carasoyn'. (The first part appeared as 'The Fairy Fleet' in *Argosy*, April, 1866.)

(4) 'The Gray Wolf'. (*Works of Fancy and Imagination*, 1871, vol.x.)

(5) 'The Cruel Painter'. (*Adela Cathcart*, 1864.)

(6) 'The Broken Swords'. (*Monthly Christian Spectator*, 1854.)

(7) 'The Wow O'Rivven [The Bell]'. (Published as 'The Bell' in *Good Words*, Feb., 1864.)

(8) 'Uncle Cornelius, His Story'. (*Works of Fancy and Imagination*, 1871.)

(9) 'The Butcher's Bills'. (*The Gifts of the Child Christ and Other Tales*, 1882.)

(10) 'Birth, Dreaming, Death [The Schoolmaster's Story]'. (*Adela Cathcart*, 1864.)
     'That Holy Thing', a Christmas poem, 1877.

Illustrations: 7 by Hughes, 5 by C. Robinson (*Illustrated London News*), and a caricature of MacDonald by Fred Walker (*Once a Week*, Nov. 2, 1872).

Issued to commemorate the centenary of MacDonald's visit to the USA in 1872–3, this is the most comprehensive collection of his short stories and fairy tales yet published, though it is not complete, as claimed in the introduction, since 'Stephen Archer' is omitted. The introduction includes a 'Letter to American Boys' (pp.10–16), 'written and published in 1878' by MacDonald: no

Sixpence Nett

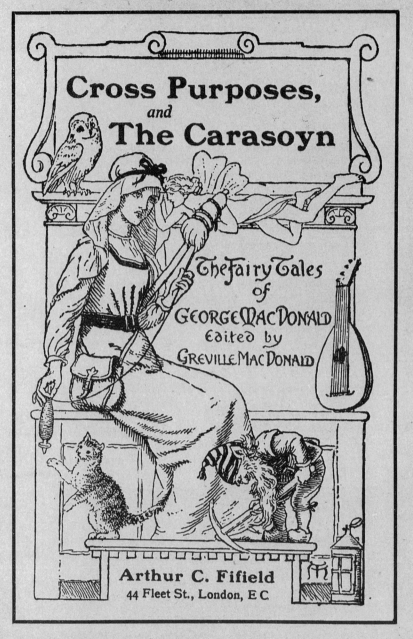

Cross Purposes,
and
The Carasoyn

The Fairy Tales
of
George MacDonald
Edited by
Greville MacDonald

Arthur C. Fifield
44 Fleet St., London, E C

10. The cover of the paperback edition of *Cross Purposes* and *The Carasoyn* (1905) with cover design by Arthur Hughes.

further details of publication are given – it is, however, listed as a separate item in this bibliography.

1882

72.   ORTS. By George MacDonald, LL.D. Sampson Low, Marston, Searle & Rivington, 1882.

8vo: pp. viii, 312, (32 adv. dated Nov., 1882). Olive-brown cloth, spine and lettering in gilt and black, plain edges.

A collection of thirteen essays, mostly reprints, with a preface signed 'G.M.D.' The title is an archaic term for 'scraps', and in the preface the author expresses doubt as to its fitting the nature of the volume. However, he defends it on the ground that the essays are 'but fragmentary presentments of larger meditation'.

Contents:
(1) 'The Imagination: its Functions and its Culture', 1867. [*British Quarterly Review*, July, 1867. The 'mathematical friend', referred to in footnote no. 4, was C. L. Dodgson.]
(2) 'A Sketch of Individual Development', 1880. [*British Quarterly Review*, Jan., 1882.]
(3) 'St. George's Day, 1564', 1864. [An essay on the tercentenary of the birth of Shakspere, as MacDonald spelt the name.]
(4) 'The Art of Shakspere as revealed by himself', 1863.
(5) 'The Elder Hamlet', 1875. [*Macmillan's Magazine*, Aug., 1876: a prelude to his *Tragedie of Hamlet*, 1885, q.v.]
(6) 'On Polish', 1865. [*Good Words*, Sept., 1865. Polish is defined as 'that condition of surface which allows the inner structure of the material to manifest itself'.]
(7) 'Browning's "Christmas Eve",' 1853 [*Monthly Christian Spectator*, May, 1853, q.v.].
(8) 'Essays on Some of the Forms of Literature', a review of the book of the same title [published 1853] by T. T. Lynch. [Thomas Toke Lynch was a writer on religious subjects, and a friend of MacDonald.]
(9) 'The History and Heroes of [the Art of] Medicine', a review of the book of the same title [published 1861] by Dr J. Rutherford Russell. [MacDonald dedicated *Adela Cathcart* (1864) to him. A sketch of Russell (1818–67) appeared in the *British Journal of Homoeopathy*, April, 1867, and was reprinted as a pamphlet.]
(10) 'Wordsworth's Poetry', delivered extempore at Manchester.
(11) 'Shelley'. [Reprinted from the article, signed 'G.M.D.', in the 1860 edition of the *Encyclopaedia Britannica*.]
(12) 'A Sermon' on Phil, iii, 15–16, read in the Unitarian Chapel, Essex Street, London, 1879. [*Unitarian Review*, Boston, Sept., 1881. A

footnote from Bordighera, July 18, 1881, stated: 'It is the only sermon I have *written* to preach for thirty years.']

(13) 'True Christian Ministering', a spoken sermon on Matt, xx, 25–8. [In the preface, MacDonald wrote: 'The title ... is not quite suitable. It is that of the religious newspaper which reported the sermon. I noted the fact too late for correction. It ought to be *True Greatness.*' This was corrected in the American edition of 1883, but not in *A Dish of Orts*, 1893, q.v.]

1883 First American publication. Published as *The Imagination and other essays*, by Lothrop & Co., Boston, USA: 8vo, pp.312. Introduction by A. P. Peabody, dated Cambridge [Mass.] Mar. 9, 1883.

[1885] Reissued by Lothrop, Boston; 12mo.

1893 An extended version was published as *A Dish of Orts*, q.v.

1882

73. WEIGHED AND WANTING. By George MacDonald, LL.D. Sampson Low, Marston, Searle & Rivington, 1882.

8vo: 3 vols: vol.I – pp.iv, 296; vol.II – pp.iv, 284; vol.III – pp.iv, 315, (1). Red cloth, gilt spine, blind-stamped covers, plain edges.

Serialised in the *Sunday Magazine*, Jan.–Dec., 1882. Reviewed in the *Athenaeum*, Nov. 4, 1882, *Saturday Review*, Nov. 25, 1882, and the *Spectator*, March 24, 1883 – all three were unfavourable.

According to Robert Lee Wolff (*The Golden Key*, pp.303, 304), the performance of 'Pilgrim's Progress' by a drunken old ex-clergyman was 'a sardonic reference [by MacDonald] to his own family performance of the same play. ... The novel's preoccupation with entertainment as an important ... social service surely reflects his effort to answer the critics of the family theatrical enterprise'.

1882 First American publication. Published by Lothrop, Boston, and by Harper, New York ('Franklin Square Library').

1883 Published by Sampson Low, pp.iv, 379.

1883 Published by Munro, New York ('Seaside Library').

1885 Published by Lothrop, Boston: illustrated.

1894 Published by Sampson Low.

[1900] Published by Richard Edward King.

1905 Published by Newnes.

1908 Published by Edwin Dalton.

1883

74. THE PRINCESS AND CURDIE. By George MacDonald, LL.D. Chatto & Windus, 1883 [1882].

8vo: pp. vi, 255, (1), (32 adv. dated Oct. 1882): frontispiece and 10 plates in line by James Allen. Pale olive-green cloth, gilt lettering, yellow edges.

Serialised in *Good Things: A Picturesque Magazine for Boys and Girls*, Jan.–June, 1877, this is a sequel to *The Princess and the Goblin* (1872). The illustrations are new, and much inferior to those by Arthur Hughes in the first 'Princess' book.

1883 First American publication. Published by Lippincott, Philadelphia, with Allen's illustrations.

1883 Published in Tauchnitz's 'Collection of British Authors', Leipzig.

[1883] Published in Munro's 'Seaside Library', New York: subtitled 'A Girl's Story'.

1888 Published by Blackie, with 8 of Allen's illustrations in tints.

1900 Published by Blackie, with illustrations by Helen Stratton.

1900 Published by Burt, New York.

1908 Published by Lippincott, Philadelphia, with 12 col. illustrations by Maria L. Kirk.

1912 Published by Blackie, with 12 col. plates and 29 illustrations in the text.

1914 Published by Lippincott, Philadelphia: 12mo, pp. 126. A simplified version by Elizabeth Lewis, with col. illustrations by Maria L. Kirk.

1926 Published by McKay, Philadelphia: col. illustrations by Gertrude A. Kay.

1927 Published by Saalfield, New York, illustrated by Frances Brundage.

1927 Published by Macmillan, New York, illustrated by Dorothy P. Lathrop. Reprinted 1942.

1934 Published by McKay, Philadelphia (reprint of 1926 edition).

1949 with reprints to 1973 Published by Dent, London, and Dutton, New York, with 8 col. plates and line drawings by Charles Folkard.

1954 Published by Macmillan, New York, illustrated by Nora S. Unwin.

Mabel Baldock.
from Mother Dec 30. 84.

THE PRINCESS AND

CURDIE

BY

GEORGE MACDONALD, LL.D.

WITH ELEVEN ILLUSTRATIONS BY JAMES ALLEN

London

CHATTO & WINDUS, PICCADILLY

1883

[*All rights reserved*]

11.   Title page of the first edition of *The Princess and Curdie* (1883).

1956 Published by Collins, illustrated by Will Nickless.

1960 Published by Random House, New York ('Looking Glass Library'): illustrated by Helen Stratton.

1966 with reprints to 1973   Published by Penguin Books: illustrated by Helen Stratton.

1970 Published by American Education Publications, Middletown, Conn., together with *The Princess and the Goblin*: abridged by Olive Jones. Illustrations (part col.) by William Stobbs.

1970 Published by Collins, together with *The Princess and the Goblin*: abridged.

1973 Published by Blackie.

1883

75.   A THREEFOLD CORD: Poems by Three Friends. Edited by George MacDonald. Not to be had of any bookseller, but by application to Mr. W. Hughes, 43, Beaufort Street, Chelsea, London. Price Five Shillings.

16mo; pp.iv, 349, (3 blank, apart from imprint of Unwin Brothers, Printers, Chilworth and London, on p.[351]). Red cloth, printed paper label on spine, uncut edges. Some copies have a pink paper slip tipped in between the front endpapers, bearing the following:

> 'This volume is now to be obtained
> from Messrs. Chatto & Windus, London;
> and from all Booksellers. Only a limited
> number are for sale.'

It is not known how many copies were sold thus, but the book was still being advertised by Chatto & Windus in 1906.

In the above copy, the title page is 5½ins×3½ins. Bulloch states that he examined Greville MacDonald's copy, and gives dimensions of 5¼ins×3¼ins without further specification. He gives the pagination as viii, 349, (7); the paper as pink; and does not mention the inserted slip. The British Museum copy, acquired in 1949, has plain cut edges: the title page is 5½ins×3⁵⁄₁₆ins, and is inscribed 'To my beloved friend John Ruskin – George MacDonald'. It has no inserted slip, but otherwise corresponds to the first description.

Dedication (p.iii) to Greville Matheson MacDonald, MD, in the form of a sonnet, signed George MacDonald and dated Casa Coraggio, May, 1883. It begins–

> 'First, most, to thee, my son, I give this book,
> In which a friend's and brother's verses blend

Margaret Vivien White
with love from

A THREEFOLD CORD:

George MacDonald

Feb. 28, 1888.

Bordighera POEMS

BY THREE FRIENDS.

EDITED BY

GEORGE MAC DONALD.

Not to be had of any bookseller, but by application to

MR. W. HUGHES, 43, BEAUFORT STREET,
CHELSEA, LONDON.

———

PRICE FIVE SHILLINGS.

12.   Title page of the first edition of *A Threefold Cord* (1883).

> With mine; for not son only – brother, friend
> Art thou . . .'

The brother was John Hill MacDonald (d.1858); the friend, Greville Ewing Matheson (d.1872), after whom MacDonald's eldest son was named. However, it is not possible to identify the poems in every case, since the book has neither table of contents nor index, and the poems are all unsigned. According to Joseph Johnson, 'more than sixty of the poems were composed by MacDonald, twenty-two by Greville Matheson, and the rest by John Hill MacDonald' (*George MacDonald*, 1906, p.61). The book contains a total of 182 poems excluding the dedicatory sonnet; many are untitled, and very few are dated.

Some of the poems by George MacDonald had previously appeared in novels ('The Laverock' in *Sir Gibbie*, 'The Old Garden' in *Donal Grant*, etc.), and in periodicals ('The Wind and the Moon' and 'The Foolish Harebell' in *Good Words for the Young*, etc). Most of Greville Ewing Matheson's poems had been copied by George MacDonald onto 17 thin quarto cards, bound to form an album, and decorated with ferns, ivy, and autumn leaves in watercolour by Mrs. MacDonald; it came into the possession of Greville MacDonald, who describes it in the *Life*, p.157. John Hill MacDonald appears in *Robert Falconer*, which also includes some of his verses. His portrait faces p.161 in the *Life*, which contains numerous references to him and to Greville Ewing Matheson.

Almost all the poems in this collection were reprinted in *The Poetical Works*, 1893, vol.ii, in altered form. The title is taken from Ecclesiastes, 4, xii: '. . . a threefold cord is not quickly broken'.

1884   Published by Alexander Strahan as *A Threefold Chord* (sic). The title page, in black and red, bears Strahan's anchor device; 'Poems by Three Friends' and '25 Henrietta Street, Covent Garden' are in red. Bound in olive-green cloth; top edge, front cover and spine in gilt. The front cover has a pictorial design of a bird enclosed in a circle, presumably to illustrate 'The Laverock'. The vellum spine bears an ornamental device embodying a harp, no doubt to echo the 'chord' in the new title. This edition uses the same typesetting, and is identical, as to dimensions, with the orginal edition.

    Whether Strahan misread the original title, or deliberately changed it, is a matter for conjecture. It is tempting to describe this as 'the first trade edition' if it were not for the fact that only one copy of this edition has been recorded, i.e. in this bibliography; it is now in a private collection. The British Library does not have a copy. It is also possible that this is a trial issue.

1883

76.   DONAL GRANT. By George MacDonald, LL.D. Kegan, Paul, Trench & Co. 1883.

8vo: 3 vols: vol.I – pp.vi, 289 (3), (39 adv. dated 10/83); vol.II – pp.vi, 289, (3); vol.III – pp.vi, 313, (3). Red cloth, spine in gilt and black, covers stamped with black borders, publisher's device in black on back cover, plain edges. Price 31s. 6d.

Donal Grant first appeared in *Sir Gibbie* (1879). In this story he is a tutor in an old country house, a situation resembling that of *The Portent* (1860). The book has much to say of Huntly and Bogieside (Bulloch, p.19).

1883   First American publication. Published by Harper, New York.

1883   Published by Lothrop, Boston.

1884   Published by Kegan Paul. 'Second Edition'. 8vo: pp.vii, (i), 397, (3), (40 adv.), with frontispiece by H.M. P[aget].

[1884] Published in Munro's 'Seaside Library', New York.

[189?] Published by Burt, New York.

1892   Published Kegan Paul, pp.406.

[n.d.] Published by Kegan Paul, pp.397. 'New Edition'.

1900   Published by Kegan Paul, pp.406.

1901   Published by Newnes, pp.viii, 250, in double columns, with Paget's illustration of 1884 on the cover. Price 6d.

1884

77.   [Preface to] LETTERS FROM HELL given in English by L.W.J.S. With a preface [pp.v–ix] by George MacDonald, LL.D. Richard Bentley & Son, 1884.

8vo: pp.x, 348.

This novel is in the form of 'letters' from a spirit who has entered the nether regions. MacDonald begins his preface:

> 'The book, of which this is an English rendering, appeared in Denmark eighteen years ago, and was speedily followed by an English translation, now long out of print, issued by the publishers of the present version. In Germany it appeared very recently in a somewhat modified form, and has there aroused almost unparalleled interest, running, I am told, through upwards of twelve editions in the course of a year. The present English version is made from this German

version, the translator faithfully following the author's powerful conception, but pruning certain portions, recasting certain others, and omitting some less interesting to English readers, in the hope of rendering such a reception and appreciation as the book itself deserves, yet more probable in this country.

It may be interesting to some to know that the title is not quite a new one, for just before the death of Oliver Cromwell a book was published entitled *Messages from Hell*; or *Letters from a Lost Soul*. This I have not had the opportunity of looking into; but it must be a remarkable book, I do not say, if it equals, but if it comes halfway toward the fearful interest of this volume.

My sole motive towards offering to write a preface to the present form of the work was my desire to have it read in this country. In perusing the German a few months ago, I was so much impressed with its imaginative energy, and the power of truth in it, that I felt as if, other duties permitting, I would gladly have gone through the no slight labour of translating it myself . . .' (pp.v, vi).

Reprinted 1885, 1889 ('New and Cheaper Edition').

1885

78. THE TRAGEDIE OF HAMLET, PRINCE OF DENMARKE, a study with the text of the Folio of 1623. By George MacDonald. [Motto]: 'What would you, gracious figure?' [Motto, and 'HAMLET, PRINCE OF DENMARKE' printed in red]. Longmans, Green & Co. 1885.

8vo: pp.xiv, 277, (1), (24 adv. dated April, 1884). Black cloth, front cover and spine in red, plain edges. Price 12s. Dedication, dated Bordighera, Christmas, 1884, to 'My honoured relative, Alexander Stewart MacColl, a little *less* than kin [he was the brother of Mac-Donald's step-mother], and a little *more* than kind, to whom I owe in especial the true understanding of the great soliloquy . . .'

The text is printed on the left-hand pages, with comments on the right. In the preface, MacDonald writes:

'My theory is – that Shakspere worked upon his own copy of the Second Quarto, cancelling and adding, and that, after his death, this copy came, along with original manuscripts, into the hands of his friends the editors of the Folio, who proceeded to print according to his alterations.'

MacDonald lectured on 'Hamlet' in the early 1870's, and contributed an essay, 'The Elder Hamlet', to *Macmillan's Magazine*, August, 1876 (reprinted in *Orts*, 1882, and *A Dish of Orts*, 1893). In a letter to his friend and literary agent, A. P. Watt, dated Bordighera, Feb. 26, 1885, MacDonald wrote:

> 'As I expected, the critics are down on my *Hamlet* on all sides. Of course! They are just of the class that cannot understand him or his inventor' (*Life*, p.541).

Greville MacDonald, who came into possession of the manuscript (Bulloch, p.46), believed it would come to be recognised as 'the most important interpretation of the play ever written' (*Life*, p.540). This view was endorsed by Sir Johnston Forbes-Robertson, in his introduction to the 1924 edition (see below).

According to Joseph Johnson (*George MacDonald*, 1906, p.170), this was the only book of MacDonald's to be published on a royalty basis, and the only one that did not make a profit.

1905 Published by Arthur C. Fifield, cheap edition, demy 8vo, pp.278, cloth, price 2s.

1924 Centenary Edition, published by George Allen & Unwin, pp.xvi, 277, (1), with a photograph of MacDonald in old age as frontispiece, and an introduction (p.vii) by Sir Johnston Forbes-Robertson. An adaptation of MacDonald's bookplate appears on the dust-wrapper and half-title. Printed in Saxony, price 8s. 6d.

Forbes-Robertson was a friend of the MacDonalds (see his memoirs, *A Player under Three Reigns*, 1925), His introduction (p.vii) begins:

> 'Of all the books and pamphlets on Hamlet that have come under my notice . . . this study by George MacDonald is by far and away the most erudite and scholarly.'

It ends with a personal tribute to MacDonald.

1885

79. UNSPOKEN SERMONS, Second Series. By George MacDonald. Longmans, Green & Co. 1885.

8vo: pp.viii, 317, (1), (1 adv.), (1), (12 adv. dated July, 1884). Brown cloth, gilt spine ('G. MacDonald, MA'), plain edges. On the title page is printed in red Ἔπεα Ἄπτερα ('Wingless Words') and [Motto] 'Comfort ye, comfort ye my people'. Dedication (p.vii) – 'These also after eighteen years to my wife. Casa Coraggio, Bordighera, January, 1885.' There is no table of contents in the British Museum copy.

A collection of 12 sermons, all except no.10 on New Testament texts: (1) The Way; (2) The Hardness of the Way; (3) The Cause of Spiritual

Stupidity; (4) The Word of Jesus on Prayer; (5) Man's Difficulty concerning Prayer; (6) The Last Farthing; (7) Abba, Father!; (8) Life; (9) The Fear of God; (10) The Voice of Job; (11) Self-Denial; (12) The Truth in Jesus.

1886   Published by Longmans.

1886

80.   WHAT'S MINE'S MINE. By George MacDonald. Kegan Paul, Trench & Co, 1886.

8vo: 3 vols.: vol.I – pp.viii, 308, vol.II – pp.viii, 308, vol.III – pp.viii, 303, (1), (44 adv. dated 3.86). Light scarlet cloth, spine in gilt and black, covers with black borders, publisher's device in black on back cover, plain edges.

As in *Robert Falconer* (1868), the author's brother John Hill MacDonald appears, this time as 'Ian'. John had been in Russia from 1853 to 1855: one of his letters to his father describing a wolf-hunt is reproduced in ch.14. The escape from death, related by Ian in ch.22, is also based on one of John's Russian experiences. Greville MacDonald 'strongly suspected' that the sonnet in ch.22 was composed by John. (See the chapter entitled 'The Three Brothers', in the *Life*.) The novel has a Scottish setting. Reviewed in the *Athenaeum*, June 5, 1886.

1886   Published by Kegan Paul, Trench, in one vol. ('Second Edition'), with a woodcut frontispiece signed G.B.: pp.vi, 387, (1), (44 adv. dated 8.86).

1886   (a) Published by Routledge, New York; (b) Munro, New York ('Seaside Library'); (c) Harper, New York ('Franklin Square Library'); and (d) Lothrop, Boston.

[n.d.; *c.*1890]   Published by Kegan Paul ('New Edition'): pp.vi, 387, (1).

1892   Published by Kegan Paul.

1900   Published by Kegan Paul price 1*s.* 6*d.*

[n.d.]   Published by Burt, New York, and Crowell, New York.

1886

81.   AN OLD STORY. Single-sheet poem. Reproduced from MS author's presentation copy (British Library).

1887

82. HOME AGAIN. By George MacDonald. Kegan Paul, Trench & Co, 1887.

8vo: pp.vi, 313, (3), (44 adv. dated 8.86). Red cloth, spine and front cover in gilt and black, back cover in black, plain edges. With a frontispiece by H.M. P[aget].

Joseph Johnson gives a long synopsis of this novel in his *George MacDonald*, 1906, pp.252–5, describing it as 'a parable of a soulless woman'.

1888   First American publication. Published by Appleton, New York ('Authorised Edition').

[1888] Published by Munro, New York ('Seaside Library').

1893   Published by Kegan Paul.

1894   Published by Kegan Paul.

1902   Published by Kegan Paul price 1*s*. 6*d*.

[1911] Published by Routledge, New York ('Authorised Edition').

1887

83.   [Preface to] FOR THE RIGHT. A novel by Karl Emil Franzos. Given in English by Julie Sutter. With a preface [pp.v–x] by George MacDonald, LL.D. James Clarke & Co., 1887.

8vo: pp.xii, 531.

MacDonald's preface begins:

> 'Not having even been asked to do so, I write this preface from admiration of the book. The translation I have not yet seen, but knowing previous work by the same hand, have confidence in it.'

This refers to Julie Sutter's German translation of *David Elginbrod* (1863, q.v.). The novel is set in the Carpathians.

1889   'New Edition', pp.viii, 278; (preface pp.iii–vi); double columns. This edition includes an extract from a review in *The Nineteenth Century* by W. E. Gladstone.

[1887]

84. 'INDIAN AND COLONIAL SERIES.' From 1887 Kegan Paul, Trench, Trübner & Co. brought out the above series of 35 titles, which included 15 by MacDonald.

8vo, cream paper-covered boards with acanthus decoration in red and black, lettering in black. The front cover bears the date 1887, title-page undated. On the back cover is a numbered list of titles; those by MacDonald are:

1. *Malcolm*	17. *Annals of a Quiet Neighbourhood*
2. *The Marquis of Lossie*	19. *The Elect Lady*
4. *Donal Grant*	21. *The Seaboard Parish*
5. *Home Again*	26. *Wilfred Cumbermede*
6. *What's Mine's Mine*	28. *Thomas Wingfold, Curate*
10. *Castle Warlock*	29. *Paul Faber, Surgeon*
15. *St. George and St. Michael*	35. *There and Back*
16. *The Flight of the Shadow*	

All items in this series are scarce, only one (*The Flight of the Shadow*) having been seen by the compiler. Bulloch does not mention them. Copies of nos. 16 and 19 are in the Houghton Library, Harvard.

1889

85. UNSPOKEN SERMONS, Third Series. By George Mac-Donald. Longmans, Green & Co., 1889.

8vo: pp. viii, 262, (2), (16 adv. dated Jan., 1889). Brown cloth, gilt spine ('G. MacDonald, MA'), plain edges. On the title page is printed in red Ἔπεα Ἄπτερα ('Wingless Words') and [Motto] 'Comfort ye, comfort ye my people'. Dedicated from Bordighera, May 3, 1889, in a four-line couplet 'To My Wife'.

A collection of 12 sermons, all except no. 7 (Psalm 52, xii) on New Testament texts: (1) The Creation in Christ; (2) The Knowing of the Son; (3) The Mirrors of the Lord; (4) The Truth; (5) Freedom; (6) Kingship; (7) Justice; (8) The Displeasure of Jesus; (10) Righteousness; (11) The Final Unmasking; (12) The Inheritance.

The three series of 'Unspoken Sermons' (1867, 1885, 1889) were advertised in Longman, Green's catalogue for 1897, price 3s. 6d. each.

13.   The cover of one of the *Indian and Colonial Series* (1887).

1889

86.   THERE AND BACK by Dr. George Macdonald (sic). Serialised in *The Sun* (Alexander Gardner, Paisley and London), Sept. 7, 1889–Aug. 30, 1890. Published in book form in 1891.

1889

87.   A ROUGH SHAKING. By George MacDonald. Serialised in *Atalanta* (Trischler & Co.), Oct., 1889–Sept., 1890. Published in book form in 1891.

1891

88.   THERE AND BACK. By George MacDonald. Kegan Paul, Trench, Trübner & Co. [March or April], 1891.

8vo: 3 vols: vol. I – pp. viii, 346, (2); vol. II – pp. vi,. 348; vol. III – pp. vi, 321, (3). Serialised in *The Sun*, 1889–90 (q.v., 1889). Pale red cloth, gilt spine, black borders on front cover, black bands on spine, blind-stamped borders and publisher's device on rear cover. Plain edges. Dedication, dated Bordighera, Feb., 1891: 'In the sure hope of everlasting brotherhood, I offer this book to Ronald MacDonald, my son and friend, my pupil, fellow-student, and fellow-workman.'

On p. 321, vol. III, appears the following note:

> 'Some of the readers of this tale will be glad to know that the passage with which it ends is a real dream; and that, with but three or four changes almost too slight to require acknowledging, I have given it word for word as the friend to whom it came set it down for me.'

It gives the clue to the title of the book, which refers to the realm of the dream (a vision of God) and the return of the waking world.

This was the last of MacDonald's novels to be published in three volumes: in it reappears Thomas Wingfold, of *Thomas Wingfold, Curate* (1876).

1891   Published in 1 vol. by Kegan Paul ('Second Edition'), pp. viii, 392. The dedication is omitted, and the note, given above, is transferred to p[v].

[1891] First American publication. Published by Lothrop, Boston.

1893   Published by Kegan Paul.

1902   Published by Kegan Paul.

1891

89.　A ROUGH SHAKING. By George MacDonald. Blackie & Son, 1891. [Dec., 1890.]

8vo: pp.384 (32 adv.). Brown cloth, with pictorial front cover and spine in gilt, black and dark green. All edges olive green. Frontispiece plus eleven page illustrations by W. Parkinson. Price 6s. Dedication, dated Hampstead, August 26, 1890, to 'my great-nephew Norman MacKay Binney, aged seven, because his Godfather and Godmother love him dearly'.

The title applies, both literally and symbolically, to an earthquake (described in ch.3) and to the trials and adventures of a boy who is separated from his parents by the disaster, in which his mother dies: he is eventually reunited with his father.

> 'He had had a rough shaking. The earthquake had come and gone, and come again and gone a many times. But the shaking earth was his nurse, and she taught him to dwell in a world that cannot be shaken' (p.384).

The MacDonalds actually experienced a severe earthquake while at their home in Bordighera, in February, 1887. This is described in extracts from letters, in the *Life*, pp.513–15.

1890　First American publication. Published by Routledge, New York.

1891　Published by Lothrop, Boston.

1900　Published by Blackie.

1904　Published by Burt, New York.

1922　Published by Blackie.

1891

90.　THE FLIGHT OF THE SHADOW. By George MacDonald. Kegan Paul, Trench, Trübner & Co., 1891.

8vo: pp.viii, 337, (3), (32 adv.). Red cloth, spine and front cover in gilt and black, back cover in black, plain edges. With a frontispiece by G[ordon] B[rowne].

The 'shadow' of the title refers to 'the shadow of love' (p.92), the perverse love of power – 'not power to do things but power to make other people do things' (p.279). The demonic Lady Cairnedge, who embodies this principle, is an anticipation of *Lilith*, the first draft of which was written in 1890. 'The worm that never dies' (ch.25) also reappears in *Lilith*, published in its final form in 1895.

1891   First American publication. Published by Appleton, New York.

1894   Published by Kegan Paul.

1902   Published by Kegan Paul, price 1s. 6d.

[1911] Published by Routledge, New York, with *Home Again* (1887).

1892

91.   [Extracts from Sir Philip Sidney, edited by Mac-Donald]. A CABINET OF GEMS, CUT AND POLISHED BY SIR PHILIP SIDNEY; NOW FOR THE MORE RADIANCE PRESENTED WITHOUT THEIR SETTING BY GEORGE MACDONALD. Elliot Stock ['Elizabethan Library'], 1892.

8vo: pp.xii, 204, with frontispiece portrait of Sidney. Preface (pp.vii–ix) dated Bordighera, Jan., 1891. The extracts are mostly from *The Countess of Pembroke's Arcadia*; there are also some Psalms translated by her from the Hebrew, some passages on Sidney by Matthew Roydon, and extracts from *The Life of the renowned Sir Philip Sidney* by Lord Brooke.

In his preface, MacDonald writes:

'In making these extracts, I have taken the following liberties: I have made shorter sentences out of long ones, purely by omission: and I have, in a few places, substituted a word necessary, because of such omission, to bring out the sense.'

A note (p.ii) says: 'It is proposed to issue a second volume of *Gems from Sir Philip Sidney* later on.' This was never published.

Around 1854, MacDonald lectured on Sidney; his wife and some of her friends copied out passages from the *Arcadia*, and also helped with research at public libraries (*Life*, p.220).

1892

92.   THE HOPE OF THE GOSPEL. By George MacDonald. Ward, Lock, Bowden and Co. 1892.

8vo: pp.viii, 240, (8 adv.). Dark green cloth, gilt spine and front cover, plain edges. [Motto] ὃ γέγονεν ἐν αὐτῷ ζωὴ ἦν.

A collection of 12 sermons on New Testament texts: (1) Salvation from Sin; (2) The Remission of Sins; (3) Jesus in the World; (4) Jesus and his Fellow-Townsmen; (5) The Heirs of Heaven and Earth; (6) Sorrow the

Pledge of Joy; (7) God's Family; (8) The Reward of Obedience; (9) The Yoke of Jesus; (10) The Salt and the Light of the World; (11) The Right Hand and the Left; (12) The Hope of the Universe.

The last appeared in the *Sunday Magazine*, 1892, xxi, 659–64, 770–73, and was later published, in abridged form, as a 4-page antivivisectionist pamphlet *The Hope of the Universe*, [1896] (Bulloch, p.26).

1892   First American publication. Published by Appleton, New York.

1893

93.   HEATHER AND SNOW. A Novel. By George MacDonald. Chatto & Windus, [April] 1893.

8vo: 2 vols: vol.I – pp.viii, 215, (1); vol.II – pp.viii, 215, (1), (32 adv. dated March, 1893). None of the prelims of vol.II are numbered except the last, which is given as vi instead of viii. Dark blue cloth, gilt spine, covers blind-stamped, front covers with pictorial design of heather in gilt, and snow in white. Top edge blue, others plain.

An Aberdeenshire story, completed before June 15, 1892 (*Life*, p.539).

1893   Published by Chatto & Windus in 1 vol: 8vo, pp.viii, 279, (1), (32 adv. dated July, 1893).

1893   First American publication. Published by Harper, New York.

1894   Published by Chatto & Windus.

1896   Published by Chatto & Windus.

1893

94.   A DISH OF ORTS. Chiefly papers on the Imagination, and on Shakspere. By George MacDonald, LL.D. Enlarged Edition. Sampson Low Marston & Co. MDCCCXCIII.

[On the title-page, 'A Dish of Orts' and 'London' are printed in red.] 8vo: pp.viii, 322. Blue cloth, gilt spine, plain edges. Frontispiece: heliogravure portrait of MacDonald by Lemercier, Paris, from a photograph by Elliot & Fry. Facsimile of MacDonald's signature below portrait, and blind-stamped on front cover. With a preface signed Edenbridge, Kent, Aug. 5, 1893.

Contents as in *Orts*, 1882 (q.v.), with the addition of 'The Fantastic Imagination', an essay that appeared, also in 1893, as the preface to *The Light Princess and other fairy tales*, G. P. Putnam's Sons, New York (q.v.

under *Dealings with the Fairies*, 1867): it is reprinted in the Eerdmans/ Mowbray collection, 1973 (q.v. under *The Gifts of the Child Christ*, 1882). *True Christian Ministering* reappears under the same title (q.v. *Orts*, 1882).

1895   Published by Sampson Low Marston & Co.

1905   Published by Newnes.

1908   Published by Edwin Dalton: frontispiece plus 3 page illustrations by Cyrus Cuneo and G. H. Evinson. On the title page, the spelling is altered to 'Shakespeare'.

1893

95.   THE POETICAL WORKS OF GEORGE MACDONALD. In two volumes. Chatton & Windus, 1893.

8vo: vol.I – pp.viii, 448; vol.II – pp.x, 424. Gilt spine, purple buckram, uncut edges, the binding uniform with *Rampolli*, 1897. Price 12s.

This collection of over 450 poems, though the most comprehensive published, is by no means complete. In a letter to W. Carey Davies, dated June 15, 1892, MacDonald wrote:

'... I hope, with you, I shall not have to change much in my new edition of Poems. It is very troublesome, but one cannot let wrongness of any kind willingly pass. It will be in two volumes and complete – all except the Diary [of an Old Soul], Translations, and the Poems in Phantastes . . .' (*Life*, p.539).

Greville MacDonald adds that much of his father's verses, scattered through the novels and fairy tales, are also omitted (ibid., p.540).

In essence, the collection consists of 'Within and Without' (1855), 'Poems' (1857), 'The Disciple and other poems' (1867), and 'A Threefold Cord' (1883), with additional poems, grouped as follows:

Vol.I: 'Within and Without', 'A Hidden Life', 'A Story of the Sea-Shore', 'The Disciple', 'The Gospel Women', 'A Book of Son-nets', 'Organ Songs', 'Violin Songs', 'Songs of the Days and Nights', 'A Book of Dreams', 'Roadside Poems', 'To and of Friends'.
Vol.II: 'Parables', 'Ballads', 'Minor Ditties', 'Motes in the Sun', 'Poems for Children', 'A Threefold Cord', 'Scots Songs and Ballads'.

Many of the above were included in *Works of Fancy and Imagination*, 1871 (q.v.). *A Threefold Cord*, 1883 (q.v.) includes poems not by MacDonald: it here ends with 'The Shortest and Sweetest of Songs' –

'Come
Home.'

Very few of the poems are dated, and no details are given of first publication. Bulloch traces almost 40 of these, in periodicals such as *Good Words*, *Good Words for the Young*, *Day of Rest*, *Illustrated London News*, etc. The *Scots Songs and Ballads* were reprinted separately by John Rae Smith, Aberdeen, as *Scotch Songs and Ballads*, 1893 (q.v.). Joseph Johnson devotes two chapters of his *George MacDonald* (1906) to MacDonald's poetry (pp.87–137).

1911   Reprinted by Chatto & Windus from the same type on thin paper; 2 vols; cloth, 2*s*. per vol., and leather, 3*s*. per vol.

1915   The above, in one volume. Green cloth, gilt spine, plain edges. Very scarce in this form.

1893

96.   SCOTCH SONGS AND BALLADS. By George MacDonald, LL.D. John Rae Smith, Aberdeen, 1893.

8vo, pp.(vi), vi, [134], [6], price 3*s*. 6*d*. (recorded by Bulloch from the Aberdeen University Library copy). A reprint of the *Scots Songs and Ballads* from vol. 2 of *The Poetical Works*, 1893. Bulloch notes that the Aberdeen publisher 'very characteristically uses the ugly word "Scotch"'.

1895

97.   LILITH: A ROMANCE. By George MacDonald, author of *Phantastes*. Chatto & Windus, Piccadilly, 1895. ['Lilith' and 'Chatto & Windus, Piccadilly' printed in red.]

8vo, pp.viii, 351; one page of ads of MacDonald's works on p.[ii], plus 32 pages of ads bound in after p.[352]. Black cloth, gilt spine, plain edges. Price 6*s*.

Motto (on title page): ' "Off, Lilith!" – The Kabala'. A quotation from Thoreau's essay, 'Walking', pp.[v, vi]. Table of contents, pp.[vii], viii. (Note: the motto cannot be accepted as a literal quotation, since the Kabala is a secret unpublished doctrine.)

This powerful and sombre fantasy is now regarded by many as Mac-Donald's greatest work, having certain affinities with *Phantastes* (1858). The author himself felt it to be God-inspired, though his wife was much troubled by it. The first edition was received either unfavourably or in silence, the praise of another master of fantasy, H. G. Wells, being an honourable exception (see Introduction).

Fortunately all the MS versions exist, having been donated to the British Museum by MacDonald's children Greville and Winifred (Lady Troup). Wolff was the first to report the placing of the MS (Greville, in the 1924 edition of *Lilith*, referred to 'an earlier version'). In fact there are no less than eight MS versions in the British Museum (Wolff is in error in giving only six: furthermore he omits the whole of the first paragraph when quoting the beginning of *Lilith I*). We will here summarise them as follows, using the terms MS and TS literally:

Version I: Pp.160, in MS with hardly a correction. Begun March 28, 1890. Untitled.

Version II: Pp.258, in TS with much correction in MS. Differs greatly from the above. Title, *Anacosm, A Tale of the Seventh Dimension*, crossed out and *Lilith* substituted.

Version III: Pp.459. Title in MS (p.1):
Lilith
A Romance
'Off, Lilith.'
p.2. Quote from Thoreau, in MS. Pp.3–458, TS, much corrected in MS. P.459 in MS, ending, 'But perhaps when I am most awake, I am dreaming all the time.'

Version IV: Pp.299. In TS, much corrected in MS.

Version V: Pp.222: In TS, much corrected in MS. Ends, 'Asleep or awake, I wait.'

Version VI: Proof, much corrected. Ends with quotation from Novalis, inserted in MS.

Version VII: First revise (page proofs). Stamped 'Spottiswoode & Co. [printers], 21, Jan, 1895.' Pp.349, much corrected.

Version VIII: Second revise. Pp.viii, 351, with 1 page of ads facing title page which is printed in black. Very few corrections. Half-title is inscribed in George MacDonald's hand: 'Winifrid Louisa MacDonald from her father – to close the series of development. May, 1895.' Bound in white cloth over boards.

A note attached to Version I states: 'By the desire of both Greville MacDonald MD and Lady Troup (son and daughter of the author) these papers are gratefully consigned to the care of the British Museum.
Winifred Louisa Troup,
1946.'

1895 First American publication. Published by Dodd, Mead & Co., New York: 12mo, pp.vi, 351 (Bulloch).

1896 'Second edition', Chatto & Windus. Apart from grey lettering on the spine instead of gilt, this is identical with the first edition.

1924   'Centenary edition', George Allen & Unwin. 8vo, pp.xx, 396. With a tipped-in b/white frontispiece by F. D. Bedford. The half-title has a facsimile of George MacDonald's bookplate. Red cloth, gilt lettering on spine and front cover, plain edges. An important edition which includes an 'introductory key, a paraphrase of an earlier manuscript-version, and explanation of notes, by Greville MacDonald' (title page). The novel is printed from the same plates as the first edition. The structure of the book is unbalanced, for the introduction (pp.ix–xx) comes between the table of contents of the 1895 edition (pp.[vii], viii) and the text of that edition (pp.1–351). Greville's paraphrase of the first version then follows (pp.355–96).

1954   See no.8, 1954.

1962   Published by Victor Gollancz together with *Phantastes* in one volume: see no.8, 1962. Introduction (pp.7–11) by C. S. Lewis, being a much abbreviated version of his preface to *George MacDonald: an Anthology*, 1946 (see 128). Reprinted 1971.

1964   As above, published by W. B. Eerdmans, Grand Rapids, USA.

1969   Published by Ballantine Books, London and New York, in their 'Adult Fantasy' series (paperback). Cover-to-cover design in colour by Gervasio Gallardo. Introduction by Lin Carter. 'First US printing: September, 1969.'

1971   As above, 'First UK printing: December, 1971.'

1971   Reprint of the Gollancz edition of 1962.

1897

98.   SALTED WITH FIRE. Serialised in the *Glasgow Weekly Mail*, Jan. 9–May 1, 1897, and published in book form in [Oct.] 1897.

1897

99.   RAMPOLLI: growths from a long-planted root, being translations, new and old, chiefly from the German; along with *A Year's Diary of an Old Soul*. By George MacDonald. Longmans, Green, and Co. 1897.

8vo: pp.viii, 303, (1), (32 adv. of May, 1897). Bound in purple buckram, gilt spine, uncut edges. (The binding is uniform with *The Poetical Works*,

1893. The dye used was extremely fugitive, and it is doubtful whether any copies can now be found in their original state.)

This is a revised and enlarged version of *Exotics*, 1876, together with *A Book of Strife in the form of The Diary of an Old Soul*, to give it its original title, which was first published in 1880.

The 'Preface to the Translations' (pp. v, vi) is a much-shortened version of the preface to *Exotics*. The translations are as in *Exotics*, though in a different order, with the following additions and one deletion:

Additions:
    From Novalis: 'Hymns to the Night' (1–6), pp. 3–6.
    From Novalis: 'A Parable', from *The Disciples at Saïs*, pp. 37–41.
    From Schiller: 3 poems, pp. 56–65.
Deletion:
    From Luther: 'Dame Music' (*Exotics*, p. 38).
    (Bulloch incorrectly gives four additional poems from Heine.)

The *Book of Strife* (pp. 183–302) is an unrevised reprint, minus the original dedication, and is printed on consecutive pages. It is followed by a terminatory untitled poem of 7 lines (p. 303), beginning 'Christ, who well knowest why my lips are sealed –' which did not appear in the first edition.

(?1902) Reprinted by Longmans, Green, 8vo, price 6s.

1905 Published as *The Diary of an Old Soul and translations of other spiritual verse* by Arthur C. Fifield, from the same plates as the 1897 edition. Price 2s., red cloth, gilt spine.

1897

100. SALTED WITH FIRE. By George MacDonald, LL.D. Hurst & Blackett, [Oct.] 1897.

8vo: pp. iv, 325, (1), (6+24 adv.). Dark-brown cloth, gilt spine and front cover, 4 thistles blind-stamped on front cover, plain edges.

This story of an erring minister, set in Scotland, was serialised in the *Glasgow Weekly Mail*, Jan. 9–May 1, 1897.

1897 First American publication. Published by Dodd, Mead, New York, with the subtitle 'A story of a Minister': 12mo, pp. iv, 324 (Bulloch, p. 42).

1900 Published by Hurst & Blackett.

1898

101.   FAR ABOVE RUBIES. By George MacDonald. *The Sketch*, Christmas number, 1898.

This novella was the last thing MacDonald wrote. It never appeared in book form in the UK.

[?1899]   First American publication. Published by Dodd, Mead, New York, in their 'Phoenix' series, 16mo, pp.183, price 40 cents. Beige cloth, floral design in pink and green on front cover and spine which are also stamped in black. This is the first edition.

1913   Published by Barre and Hopkins, New Jersey, in their 'Baltimore' series.

1973

102.   THE LITTLE GIRL THAT HAD NO TONGUE.

An unpublished children's story, date of composition not known, with an introduction by Glenn Edward Sadler, in vol.II, pp.18–34, of *Children's Literature: The Great Excluded*, edited by Francelia Butler. Published by the English Department, University of Connecticut. A facsimile of the MS, now in the Houghton Library, Harvard University, is given on alternate pages facing the printed text, which embodies verbatim MacDonald's corrections. Reprinted 1974.

PART III

TRANSLATIONS OF MACDONALD'S WORKS

103. [GUILD COURT, French translation]. *Lucy Burton*, translated by Emile Jouveaux. Published by F. Amyot, Paris. 8vo, pp.316. (Bulloch, p.24).

1873

103A. [DAVID ELGINBROD, German translation]. *David Elginbrod* von George MacDonald. Aus dem Englischen übersetzt von Julie Sutter. Autorisierte Uebersetzung. Verlag von Heyder & Zimmer, Frankfurt a.M.

[1958]

104. [AT THE BACK OF THE NORTH WIND, Polish translation]. *Na skrzydłach połnocnej wichury*. Ilustracje wykonała Danuta. Rewkiewicz – Niemirska. Pp.269. Published in Warsaw.

1965

105. [THE PRINCESS AND THE GOBLIN, Hebrew translation]. Published in Tel-Aviv, illustrated.

GEORGE MACDONALD

—

DIE
LACHPRINZESSIN

—

MIT ZEICHNUNGEN VON

MAURICE SENDAK

DIOGENES

14.   Dust jacket of a German translation of *The Light Princess* illustrated
by Maurice Sendak (1976).

マクドナルド童話全集**10**

北風のうしろの国

G．マクドナルド・作

田谷多枝子・訳　真島節子・絵

太平出版社

15.　Title page of a Japanese translation of *At the Back of the North Wind*
(1977).

1976

106. [THE LIGHT PRINCESS, German translation]. *Die Lach-prinzessin*. Aus dem Englischen und mit einem Nachwort von Hildegard Krahé. Mit zeichnungen von Maurice Sendak. Published by Diogenes Verlag AG Zürich.

8vo, pp.130, including a short chronology (pp.129, 130). Dark blue cloth, gilt spine, d/wrapper with illustration by Sendak on the front. Issued as a boxed set with the following item: the box has a Sendak illustration (see below).

1976

107. [THE GOLDEN KEY, German translation]. *Der Goldene Schlüssel*. Aus dem Englischen von Hildegard Krahé. Mit einem Nachwort von W. H. Auden und Zeichnungen von Maurice Sendak. Published by Diogenes Verlag AG Zürich.

8vo, pp.96. The afterword (pp.89–94) is translated by Peter Naujack. Dark blue cloth, gilt spine, d/wrapper with an illustration by Sendak on the front. Issued as a boxed set, uniform with the above item. The box has a Sendak illustration from *Der Goldene Schlüssel*.

Note: The above two items were first published in the same format, in English and with the Sendak illustrations, by Farrar, Straus and Giroux, New York; *The Golden Key* in 1967 and *The Light Princess* in 1969 (see under *Dealings with the Fairies*, 1867, in Part II).

1977

108. [AT THE BACK OF THE NORTH WIND. Japanese translation]. Published by Taihei Shuppan Sha, Tokyo.

8vo. Translated by Takiko Taniguchi, who also provides an afterword which includes photos of MacDonald and his family. Illustrations by Setsuko Majima, b/white in text, in colour on boards and d/wrapper. Pictorial boards and d/wrapper reproduce illustrations from the story. Coloured frontispiece. Reprinted 1980.

Other translations of George MacDonald's work published by Taihei Shuppan Sha, Tokyo are as follows:

(a) *Longer stories:* 'The Princess and the Goblin', 'The Princess and Curdie', 'The Lost Princess'.
(b) *Short stories:* 'The Light Princess', 'The Giant's Heart', 'The Carasoyn', 'Little Daylight', 'The Day Boy and the Night Girl', 'The Golden Key', 'The Shadows', 'Cross Purposes'.

1977

109. [PHANTASTES, Italian translation]. *Anados*, translated by Giorgio Spina. Published by Rusconi editore, Milano.

16mo, pp.216. Paperback, coloured illustration on cover. With biographical and bibliographical notes by the translator.

1981

110. [AT THE BACK OF THE NORTH WIND. German translation]. *Hinter dem Nordwind*, translated by Sybil Gräfin Schönfeld. Published by Betz, Vienna.

1983

111. [LILITH, German translation]. *Lilith*, translated by Uwe Herms. Published by Klett, Stuttgart.

1984

112. [THE DAY BOY AND THE NIGHT GIRL, German translation]. *Tagjunge und Nachtmädchen*, translated by Werner Schmitz, in the anthology *Aufstand der Elfen*, ed. Jack Zipes. Published by Diederichs, Cologne.

1984

113. [PHANTASTES, German translation]. *Phantastus: Ein Feenmärchen*, translated by Hans Günter Holl. Published by Robinson, Frankfurt.

1984

114. [THE LIGHT PRINCESS AND THE GIANT'S HEART, German translation]. *Die Lichtprinzessin und Das Herz des Riesen: Phantastische Märchen*, translated and with an afterword by Hans Günter Holl. Published by Robinson, Frankfurt.

1986

115. [GEORGE MACDONALD: AN ANTHOLOGY (1946) BY C. S. LEWIS, German translation]. *Die Weisheit meines Meisters*, translated by M. Gisi and Hans Urs Kardinal von Balthazar. Published by Einsideln, Switzerland.

1987

116. [THE GOLDEN KEY AND THE CARASOYN, Italian translation]. *Racconti: La chiave d'oro; Il nettare magico*, translated by Giorgio Spina. Published by Manganò editore, Bordighera.

16mo, paperback, pp.128. One b/white illustration on the cover and five more in the text, by Andrea Rebando. With a critical introduction by the translator.

PART IV

SELECTIONS FROM
GEORGE MACDONALD

The following items consist of books devoted entirely to extracts from MacDonald's writings. Entry no.122, however, contains only a limited amount of material by MacDonald, but is included because the compilers were members of MacDonald's family.

[1880]

117.   CHEERFUL WORDS FROM THE WRITINGS OF GEORGE MAC-DONALD. Selected by E. E. Brown with an introduction by James T. Fields. Published by D. Lothrop, Boston.

[1885]

118.   SELECTIONS FROM THE WRITINGS OF GEORGE MAC-DONALD, OR HELP FOR WEARY SOULS. Compiled by J. Dewey. Published by Thomas R. Knox, New York, 8vo.

1889   Published by F. N. Dusenberry, Chicago, 16mo.

1887

119.   GOD'S WORDS TO HIS CHILDREN; SERMONS SPOKEN AND UNSPOKEN. Published by Funk & Wagnalls, New York. Reprinted 1912.

1887

120.   POEMS BY GEORGE MACDONALD, LL.D. Selected by V.D.S. and C.F. Published by E. P. Dutton, New York. Includes two poems by MacDonald's brother John, from *Robert Falconer*.

1894

121.   BEAUTIFUL THOUGHTS FROM GEORGE MACDONALD. Arranged by Elizabeth W. Dougall. Published by James Pott, New York. Reprinted 1907.

1904

122.   BABIES' CLASSICS. Chosen by Lilia Scott MacDonald. Illustrated by Arthur Hughes. Preface by Winifred Troup. Published by Longmans, Green.

4to, pp.xii, 80.

This collection of poems contains only four by George MacDonald along with 22 other authors. It is of special interest, however, on account of the MacDonald family connection: both Lilia Scott MacDonald and Winifred Troup were daughters of George MacDonald. Winifred Troup relates, in her preface, that her sister had planned to publish a small collection of the best children's poems, but did not live to complete the task. She expresses the hope that there may be 'a place for the little collection which she began, and which I have completed in the way she proposed'. The exquisite illustrations by Hughes, in the artist's later style, contribute greatly to making this one of the most prefect books of its kind.

1905

123.   DAILY READINGS FROM GEORGE MACDONALD. Selected by James Dobson. Published by Arthur C. Fifield, Dec., 1905, reprinted Jan., 1906, 1907. The extracts are mostly of prose.

1906

124.   THE POCKET GEORGE MACDONALD. Selected by Alfred H. Hyatt from 42 of MacDonald's books. Published by Chatto and Windus, 1906, and by Small, Maynard & Co., Boston (? 1907).

A BABY SERMON

THE lightning and thunder,
They go and they come;
But the stars and the stillness
Are always at home.

GEORGE MACDONALD.

21

16. A poem by GMD with two illustrations by Arthur Hughes from *Babies' Classics* (1904).

[1909]

125.   LIGHT TO LIVE BY. Extracts from the *Unspoken Sermons*, chosen by Frances M. Nicholson. Published by T. N. Foulis, Edinburgh and London.

1913

126.   A BOOK OF LIFE FROM THE WORKS OF GEORGE MAC-DONALD. Chosen by W.L.T. and S.M.T. Published by Humphrey Milford. Contains 110 extracts arranged from birth to death.

n.d. *c.*1930

127.   GATHERED GRACE. A short selection of George Mac-Donald's poems, with a biographical sketch. Compiled by Elizabeth Yates. Foreword by Lucia C. Coulson. With wood engravings by Nora S. Unwin. Published by W. Heffer & Sons, Cambridge.

1946

128.   GEORGE MACDONALD: AN ANTHOLOGY. By C. S. Lewis. With a preface (pp.10–22) and 365 extracts, mostly from the *Unspoken Sermons*. Each extract is given a heading by the compiler. In the preface, C. S. Lewis acknowledges, in no uncertain terms, his debt to George MacDonald, referring to him as 'my master'. Published by Geoffrey Bles, 1946, 1947, 1955, and by Doubleday, New York, 1962.

n.d. *c.*1950

129.   VERSES CHOSEN FROM 'THE DIARY OF AN OLD SOUL' BY GEORGE MACDONALD. A curious pamphlet, compiled, printed and published anonymously. Pp.[16], in decorated paper wrappers. A short introduction is followed by 16 stanzas from *The Diary of an Old Soul*.

PART V

DRAMATISATIONS

1910

130.   COLIN IN FAIRYLAND. A 'Fairy Play' by G. J. Hamlen based on 'The Carasoyn' (see *Works of Fancy and Imagination*, vol.X, 1871). Music by Albert Cazabon.

8vo, pp.97+15 ads, blue pictorial wrappers, printed in black and silver. Published and printed by Bone & Hulley, Glasgow. A drawing by Muirhead Bone of their printing shop is reproduced on p.[8]. With b/white photos of cast, scenery, author and composer. Produced by the Scottish Repertory Theatre Company at the Royalty Theatre, Glasgow, in December, 1910. The producer was Kenelm Foss; Colin was played by Ruby Gray.

1926

131.   THE PRINCESS AND THE GOBLIN. Adapted from the book of that title (1872) by Grace Calvert Holland. Published by Erskine MacDonald.

8vo, pp.76, blue-grey paper boards, pale blue d/wrapper. Price 3*s.* 6*d.* There are two forewords (p.5), one being an extract from a letter by the actor Sir Johnston Forbes-Robertson dated July 17, 1925; the other is by Dr. Greville MacDonald. The play had evidently not been performed before the book was published.

[1930]

132.   THE PRINCESS AND THE GOBLINS (sic.). Adapted from *The Princess and the Goblin* (1872). Published by W. H. Baker, Boston.

PART VI

WRITINGS ABOUT
GEORGE MACDONALD

A. BIOGRAPHY, BIBLIOGRAPHY AND CRITICISM: WORKS DEVOTED WHOLLY TO GEORGE MACDONALD

1906 [1905]

133. GEORGE MACDONALD, A BIOGRAPHICAL AND CRITICAL APPRECIATION. By Joseph Johnson. Published by Sir Isaac Pitman & Sons, 1906. Reprinted 1908.

A light-weight work, but historically of interest as the first full-length study on MacDonald.

1924

134. GEORGE MACDONALD AND HIS WIFE. By Greville Mac-Donald, M.D. With an introduction by G. K. Chesterton, and 28 illustrations. Published by George Allen and Unwin [May 20] 1924. Reprinted Sept., 1924. Reprinted in facsimile by Allen and Unwin and Johnson Reprint Corp., New York, 1971.

This substantial work (pp.576) and written by George MacDonald's eldest son and is the most important biography that has so far appeared. It includes much useful bibliographical data.

1925

135.   A CENTENNIAL BIBLIOGRAPHY OF GEORGE MACDONALD. By John Malcolm Bulloch [1867–1938]. Aberdeen University Press, 1925, in an edition of 50 copies. This is a revised and extended version of the Aberdeen University Library Bulletin, Feb., 1925.

The pioneer bibliography, compiled between January and August, 1924, as the author tells us in his preface. The entries are arranged alphabetically. It is still of great value to the researcher despite numerous errors.

Reproduced in facsimile in *George MacDonald: A Bibliographical Catalog and Record*, compiled by Mary Nance Jordan, published for the Marion E. Wade Collection, Wheaton College, Wheaton, Illinois, in Fairfax, Virginia, 1984. Edition limited to 100 numbered copies.

1961

136.   THE GOLDEN KEY: A STUDY OF THE FICTION OF GEORGE MACDONALD. By Robert Lee Wolff. Published by Yale University Press, New Haven, Connecticut, 1961.

A substantial critical study, written from the psychoanalytical point of view.

1962

137.   GEORGE MACDONALD'S FICTION: A STUDY IN THE NATURE OF REALISM AND SYMBOLISM. By Richard H. Reis. Pp.viii, 161. Brown University, Providence [R.I.], USA.

A thesis, issued by University Microfilms [1967]; The British Library copy is in this form (1 reel, 35mm).

1972

138.   GEORGE MACDONALD. By Richard H. Reis. Published by Twayne Publishers, New York, 1972, in the 'Twayne's English Authors Series', no.119.

This study, which is critical of Wolff's *The Golden Key* (see above), is Jungian rather than Freudian. It is much shorter than *The Golden Key* (pp.161 and 425 respectively).

B. SELECTED REFERENCES TO GEORGE MACDONALD

1896

139. THE THEOLOGY OF MODERN FICTION. By Thomas G. Selby. Published by Charles H. Kelly. Includes a chapter on MacDonald, pp.131–72.

1896

140. POETIC IDEALS OF EDUCATION: THE 'MINISTREL' [of James Beattie] AND GEORGE MACDONALD. A lecture by Principal Sir Wm. D. Geddes, University of Aberdeen. Published by John Rae Smith, Aberdeen. Pp.29.

1898

141. C. L. DODGSON ('LEWIS CARROLL'). Stuart Dodgson Collingwood, in his *Life and Letters of Lewis Carroll* (1898), was the first to reveal the friendship between the two authors (see Appendix B: 'George MacDonald and Lewis Carroll'). Any major study of Lewis Carroll will contain references to George MacDonald, e.g. Florence Becker Lennon's biography (1945, revised 1972), *The Diaries of Lewis Carroll*, ed. R. L. Green, 2 vols, 1953, etc.

1905

142. THE BOOKMAN, Nov., 1905. Contains articles on MacDonald by James Moffatt and Mary Gray, with numerous photographs and a presentation portrait as a supplement.

1911

143. GEORGE MACDONALD: A PERSONAL NOTE. By Ronald MacDonald, included in *From a Northern Window*, pp.55–113, a collection of essays, ed. Frederick Watson, published by James Nisbet. A sympathetic and neglected study by one of George MacDonald's sons who became a novelist.

1925

144.   A PLAYER UNDER THREE REIGNS: The memoirs of Sir Johnston Forbes-Robertson, which includes a photograph of MacDonald as Macbeth (q.v. *The Tragedie of Hamlet*, 1885).

1929

145.   LETTERS TO A VICTORIAN EDITOR: HENRY ALLON, ED. OF THE BRITISH QUARTERLY REVIEW. By Albert Peel. Published by Independent Press.

Includes 8 letters from George MacDonald (pp.194–9). A prefatory note states that there were many more letters from MacDonald in Dr. Allon's collection, mostly relating to Congregationalist preaching engagements.

1932

146.   REMINISCENCES OF A SPECIALIST. By Greville Mac-Donald, M.D. Published by George Allen & Unwin.

These memoirs by the author of *George MacDonald and his Wife* contain further important material concerning George MacDonald: there are also two chapters on the Ruskin/MacDonald/Rose La Touche relationships (see also Derrick Leon's *Ruskin, the Great Victorian*, 1949). Later issues have a single printed leaf dated 1935 inserted as an addendum to p.122 – it prints a recently-discovered letter from George MacDonald to John Ruskin dated May 30, 1875 enclosed in a copy of *Alec Forbes of Howglen* inscribed to John Ruskin by MacDonald and dated May, 1865. With the letter MacDonald had enclosed a copy of the 1873 Novalis translations.

The Times Literary Supplement, March 14, 1935, published a letter from Greville MacDonald, referring to the above letter, with a quotation from it.

A section on *Lilith* and *Phantastes* (pp.320–6) includes a friendly letter from H. G. Wells to George MacDonald dated Sept. 24, 1895. 'I have been reading your Lilith with exceptional interest.' He goes on to compare *Lilith* with his own *The Wonderful Visit*, then awaiting publication.

1945

147. THE GREAT DIVORCE: A DREAM. By C. S. Lewis. Published by Geoffrey Bles.

The narrator's guide to the Heavenly Regions is none other than George MacDonald, complete with 'a strong Scotch accent', and named as such when he enters the story on p.59 '. . . my name is George Macdonald' [sic.]. There is a quotation from MacDonald on the title page.

1947

148. A VOYAGE TO WONDERLAND. By Hubert Nicholson. Published by Heinemann. A collection of essays, the title-essay of which compares the writings of George MacDonald and Lewis Carroll.

1949

149. RUSKIN, THE GREAT VICTORIAN. By Derrick Leon. Published by Routledge & Kegan Paul.

The gifted author of this substantial biography died when he was only thirty-six: the text was prepared from his first draft. It contains important references to Ruskin and MacDonald, who were great friends, and the Ruskin/Rose La Touche relationship. Leon co-operated with Greville MacDonald, who was one of the three dedicatees. The book includes a photograph of George MacDonald taken by Lewis Carroll.

1966

150. LETTERS OF C. S. LEWIS, ed. with a memoir by W. H. Lewis. Published by Geoffrey Bles.

C. S. Lewis frequently acknowledged his inspirational debt to George MacDonald. He first read *Phantastes* when he was about 17. Later he read the 1924 edition of *Lilith*, and gave his own analysis of that book in a letter to his close friend Arthur Greaves (in *They Stand Together: Letters of C. S. Lewis to Arthur Greaves, 1914–1963*, ed. W. Hooper, Collins 1979). Lewis rejected Greville MacDonald's 'nonsense about "dimensions" and "elements"', but confessed that 'Lilith is quite beyond me . . . I am so excited about it that I can hardly imagine anyone else being bored . . .'

1968

151. THE GEORGE MACDONALD COLLECTION, BRANDER LIBRARY, HUNTLY. By Muriel Hutton, pp.13–25 of *The Book Collector*, vol.17, no.1, Spring 1968, being no.XIII in the 'Unfamiliar Libraries' series. Published by The Collector, Ltd.

A description, by a former librarian, of one of the leading George MacDonald collections, situated in the town in which MacDonald was born.

Appendix A

GUSTAV HOLST'S 'PHANTASTES' SUITE

Gustav Holst was born in Cheltenham in 1874. At the age of 23 he set to music a poem from Chapter 5 of *Phantastes*, calling it 'Song to the Sleeping Lady'. Holst omitted the first 16 of the 48 lines, commencing his song with line 17, which runs, 'Rest is now filled full of beauty'.

In 1911 he composed a suite for orchestra called 'Phantastes'. It was performed on July 23, 1912 at the Queen's Hall, London, by the New Symphony Orchestra conducted by the composer. However he withdrew it after the first (and only) performance.

The Suite is in four movements, each prefaced with a literary quotation. That of the first (Prelude) is from *Phantastes*, and begins, 'The whole garden was like a carnival . . .'. The second movement (March) is prefaced with three lines from the well-known poem 'Jabberwocky' by MacDonald's friend Lewis Carroll. The other two movements are 'Sleep' and 'Dance'. In a letter to a friend Holst wrote that the music of this Suite was as much a part of him as his settings of the Vedic hymns, and likewise reflected his strong mystical inclinations. (Holst had taught himself Sanskrit.) The Phantastes Suite is important, for elements from it were later used in the 'Jupiter' movement of 'The Planets', in the Dance of the Spirits of Water from 'The Perfect Fool', and in other works.

Earlier Holst had made sketches for the first scene of an opera entitled 'The Magic Mirror', based on the story of Cosmo in Chapter 13 of *Phantastes*. According to Imogen Holst, the libertto was probably by Fritz B. Hart. There are several versions of the introduction and opening scene. A musical quotation dated September 25, 1896 is given in the *Thematic Catalogue* p.235 (see below). None of the above pieces by Holst have been published.

There are other MacDonald associations with Gustav Holst. After the MacDonald family left their house in Hammersmith (The Retreat), it was bought by William Morris. It became the headquarters of the Hammersmith Socialist Society, and Holst attended lectures given there by Morris, George Bernard Shaw and others. (Holst set to music some poems by Morris.) These lectures were held in the long room in which the MacDonalds had presented their theatricals. In that same room Holst conducted the newly-formed Hammersmith Socialist Choir, and dedicated his 'Song to the Sleeping Lady' to one of the sopranos, Isobel Harrison. They married in 1901, and to their only child Imogen, who died on March 9, 1984 aged 76, we are indebted for these and other musical and biographical data concerning her illustrious father.

Sources (Dates are of first editions)
1. *Gustav Holst* by Imogen Holst. Oxford University Press, 1938.
2. *A Thematic Catalogue of Gustav Holst's Music* by Imogen Holst. Faber Music, 1974.
3. *Holst* by Imogen Holst. Faber & Faber's 'Great Composers' Series, 1974.

R.B.S.

Appendix B

GEORGE MACDONALD AND LEWIS CARROLL

Abbreviations
Unless otherwise specified, *Sylvie and Bruno* refers to the two volumes,
Sylvie and Bruno (1889) and *Sylvie and Bruno Concluded* (1893).
Collingwood: *The life and Letters of Lewis Carroll*, by Stuart Dodgson
              Collingwood; T. Fisher Unwin, 1898.
GMD & Wife: *George MacDonald and his Wife*, by Greville MacDonald;
              Allen & Unwin, 1924.
Reminiscences: *Reminiscences of a Specialist*, by Greville MacDonald; Allen
              & Unwin, 1932.
Diaries: *The Diaries of Lewis Carroll*, edited by Roger Lancelyn
              Green; Cassell, 1953.
A Voyage to Wonderland is the title-essay of a collection by Hubert
Nicholson, published by Heinemann 1947. This perceptive yet little-
known essay appears to have been the first to explore the relationship
between the imaginative writings of Lewis Carroll and George Mac-
Donald.

I am indebted to Mrs. Freda Levson for the information that Professor
James Legge (1815–97) was Huntly born and related to George Mac-
Donald and that they probably met.

Grateful acknowledgements are due to the authors and publishers of
works referred to in the text.

I

FRIENDSHIP

In October, 1856, the MacDonald family went to Algiers. The visit was
undertaken for health reasons – George MacDonald suffered from
bronchial ailments – and was made possible by the generosity of Lady

Byron, who had been much impressed by MacDonald's first published book, *Within and Without*, a drama in blank verse which appeared in 1855. On their return in April, 1857, the family moved to Hastings, and took up residence in a house in the then unfashionable Tackleway, near All Saints. A glimpse into the MacDonald's home at this time was recorded by a visitor:

> I was delightfully received by a strikingly handsome young man and a most kind lady, who made me feel at once at home. There were five children at that time, all beautifully behaved and going about the house without troubling anyone. On getting better acquainted with the family, I was much struck by the way in which they carried on their lives with one another. At a certain time in the afternoon, you would, on going up-stairs to the drawing room, see on the floor several bundles – each one containing a child! On being spoken to they said, so happily and peacefully, 'We are resting', that the intruder felt she must immediately disappear. The nurse was with them. One word from the father or mother was sufficient to bring instant attention. . . . In the evenings, when the children were all in bed, Mr. MacDonald would still be writing in his study – 'Phantastes' it was – and Mrs. MacDonald would go down and sit with her husband, when he would read to her what he had been writing; and I would hear them discussing it on their return to the drawing room. To hear his reading Browning's 'Saul' with his gracious and wonderful power was a thing I shall never forget. Mrs. MacDonald's energy and courage were untiring, and her capabilities very unusual.   (*GMD & Wife*, p.289)

A friend of the MacDonalds at Hastings was Dr. Hale, a homoeopathic doctor. He, in turn, knew Dr. James Hunt, a leading authority on stammering, who lived at nearby Ore. One of his patients was Lewis Carroll, who also used to visit his aunts, the Misses Lutwidge, at Hastings. Thus Lewis Carroll came to be introduced to the Mac-Donalds, though we do not know exactly when this took place. Carroll's diaries for this period are missing. However, Greville MacDonald tells us that MacDonald's friendship with Carroll dated from the days of the Tackleway (*GMD & Wife*, p.301). The MacDonalds moved from Hastings to London in October, 1859, and so the first meeting must have taken place between the spring of 1858 and the autumn of 1859.

Outwardly, Lewis Carroll and George MacDonald differed in many respects. Carroll's background was English High Church, he was a bachelor, and was already settled as Mathmatical Lecturer at Christ Church, Oxford, where he was to reside for the rest of his life. MacDonald's background was Scottish Calvinism, he was married with a growing family (he was to have eleven children), and constantly changing residence. He was highly effective as a public speaker: Carroll was quite the reverse (only towards the end of his life did Carroll speak in public with some confidence). The MacDonalds often entertained large gatherings at home: Carroll was excessively shy in a crowd. Mark Twain once met Lewis Carroll at the MacDonalds, and recorded his impressions in his autobiography (1906, vol. 2, p. 232):

> We met a great many other interesting people, among them Lewis Carroll, author of the immortal 'Alice' – but he was only interesting to look at, for he was the stillest and shyest full-grown man I have ever met except 'Uncle Remus'. Doctor MacDonald and several other lively talkers were present, and the talk went briskly on for a couple of hours, but Carroll sat still all the while except that now and then he asked a question. His answers were brief. I do not remember that he elaborated any of them.

But what Carroll and MacDonald had in common was more impor-
tant than their differences. Both showed in their work influences of the German and English Romantics, whose common theme of an under-ground realm inhabited by gnomes and goblins could have found a reflection in *Alice's Adventures Under Ground*, and in MacDonald's two *Princess* books and others.

Both were deeply-committed Christians, with an aversion to irrever-ence, though they were by no means always solemn.

> My father, wrote Greville, who hated any touch of irreverence could laugh till tears ran at his friend's ridicule of smug formalism and copy-book maxims.   (*GMD & Wife*, p. 343)

Both loved animals and wrote against the growing practice of vivisection. A part of MacDonald's novel, *Paul Faber, Surgeon*, was reprinted as an anti-vivisectionist pamphlet.

Both were believers in homoeopathy – in George MacDonald's case, as early as 1850, as a recently-discovered letter shows, and his wife shared his enthusiasm. In *The Rectory Umbrella*, Carroll poked fun at homoeopathy – but that was before he met the MacDonalds. Later, in the diaries, we find numerous references to various homoeopathic remedies that Carroll took, and which he claimed were effective. We have already noted that a homoeopathic doctor was instrumental in bringing Carroll and the MacDonalds together. MacDonald dedicated a novel, *Adela Cathcart*, to John Rutherford Russell, physician to the Homoeopathic Hospital in London. (In an unpublished diary entry, dated July 30, 1863, Carroll recorded that he met Dr. Russell.)

Then there was the theatre. Carroll was a life-long theatre-goer. The MacDonalds went one better, and formed their own theatrical company, with a repertoire including *The Three Bears* (with George MacDonald as Father Bear) and *The Pilgrim's Progress*. In *Beauty and the Beast*, Greville relates that his father played the Beast with such pathos that he made the children cry. A photograph of George MacDonald as Macbeth forms one of the illustrations in his friend Sir Johnston Forbes-Robertson's memoirs (1925). The MacDonald company later performed in public, with their daughter Lilia as star (she had a genuine talent for acting, and turned down an offer of marriage because it was made conditional on her leaving the stage). Mrs. MacDonald published a collection of plays for children in 1870.

The MacDonalds were thus an unusual and gifted family. Greville, after a slow start at school, became an eminent nose and throat surgeon, and published fairy tales and works on medicine and philosophy. Another son, Ronald, wrote several novels. George MacDonald himself produced some 50 books, comprising poems, novels, criticism, sermons, fairy tales, and two highly original fantasies for adults, *Phantastes* and *Lilith*. He was also for a time editor of the periodical *Good Words for the Young* in which many of his best-known fairy tales first appeared. He began his career as Congregationalist Minister in Arundel, Sussex, but was forced to resign, his views having been considered too unorthodox. He then gave up preaching, professionally, and concentrated on writing. And it was in his writing, especially in his expression of the dream-vision, that he came closest to sharing – and influencing – the dream-vision of his friend Lewis Carroll.

It did not take Carroll long to make friends with the children. The earliest surviving reference by Carroll to the MacDonalds is a diary entry for 1860. It tells of a meeting with Greville and Mary, in the studio of the sculptor Alexander Munro, for whom Greville was sitting as a model for the fountain group, 'Boy Riding a Dolphin' (now in Regent's Park, London).

> They were a girl and boy, about 7 and 6 years old, I claimed their acquaintance, and began at once proving to the boy, Greville, that he had better take the opportunity of having his head changed for a marble one. The effect was that in about 2 minutes they had entirely forgotten that I was a total stranger, and were earnestly arguing the question as if we were old acquaintants. (*Collingwood*, p.85)

Carroll often took the children out for treats, visiting the Polytechnic to see the entrancing 'dissolving views' (a kind of magic lantern show introduced from France soon after 1800 and known as *Phantasmagoria*, from which Carroll got the title for his first book of poems, published in 1869), followed by cakes and ginger beer, and gifts of toys. His letters to Lilia and Mary MacDonald are the earliest of his numerous letters to child-friends.

In the 1860's, Carroll saw the MacDonalds frequently, taking numerous photographs. On July 31, 1863, he recorded in his diary:

> I have now done all the MacDonalds.

In the late seventies, the MacDonalds settled in Bordighera, on the Italian Riviera. They made regular trips to England, but Carroll gradually lost touch with them. On June 12, 1879, he wrote to Lily:

> I have been living for a very long time in the belief that you were all in Italy, and only learned the fact of your being in England, a few days ago, from Miss Willets, step-daughter of Professor Legge (our

Chinese Professor). Please send a line to tell me how you all are, and specially Mrs. MacDonald, who was too ill to see me when I called (it seems a long time ago now) at the house in Hammersmith, and saw only Greville and Winnie.

Lily was then 27. The last references to the MacDonalds are for Sept., 1882, when he took two girls to see the MacDonalds perform in Brighton '... and afterwards had a short interview with Mr. and Mrs. MacDonald', and for Nov. 6, 1882, when he invited Ronald MacDonald, then an undergraduate at Trinity, to a tête-à-tête dinner at Christ Church.

Carroll's friendship with the MacDonalds thus extended for more than twenty years, and was at its most intimate during the crucial period immediately before and during the writing of the *Alice* books. But before passing on to this aspect, we must not forget a little souvenir of Hastings that Carroll included in *Rhyme? and Reason?* (1883). One verse begins:

> For I have friends who dwell by the coast –
> Pleasant friends they are to me!

This poem first appeared in *College Rhymes*, 1861; a revised version was included in *Rhyme? and Reason?*. The original version included a stanza beginning:

> Once I met a friend in the street,
> With wife and nurse and children three:

which considerably strengthens the association of this poem with the MacDonalds.

II

INFLUENCES

Lewis Carroll first met George MacDonald around the time of the publication of *Phantastes* (Oct., 1858) or shortly after. We can be sure that Carroll read this book – in later diary entries, other books by MacDonald are mentioned. Certain passages in *Phantastes* undoubtedly influenced the *Alice* books, as the following quotations will show:

(a) *The White Rabbit and the descent underground*
   In *Phantastes* ch.17 we find the hero going down a perpendicular hole 'like a roughly excavated well' and then along a horizontal passage. He is searching, not for a white rabbit, but for a white lady. But in ch.5 he had indeed met a white rabbit – 'a large white rabbit with red eyes', and one is also mentioned in ch.3.

(b) *The Mirror Image*
   What a strange thing a mirror is! And what a wondrous affinity exists between it and a man's imagination! For this room of mine,

as I behold it in the glass, is the same and yet not the same. It is not the mere representation of the room I live in, but it looks just as if I were reading about it in a story I like. All its commonness has disappeared. The mirror has lifted it out of the region of fact into the realms of art. . . . I should like to live in that room if I could only get into it. (ch.13)

All mirrors are magic mirrors. The commonest room is a room in a poem when I turn to the glass. (ch.10)

(c) *Snowdrop*, a flower-fairy (ch.3)
Mary MacDonald had a white kitten named Snowdrop, which is also the name of the white kitten in *Through the Looking-Glass*.

'Lily', the White Pawn in *Through the Looking-Glass*, was named after the first of the MacDonald children, who was, in turn, named after the child in *Within and Without*.

Almost forty years after *Phantastes* came *Lilith*, another allegory of a quest cast in rich symbolic imagery. In *Lilith* the hero actually begins his dream-journey through a looking-glass, which he finds in a garret (ch.2).

Let us return to the Tackleway, to another sphere of interest shared by Carroll and MacDonald – the occult, a term which, in its widest sense, embraces all manner of psychical and supernatural phenomena, including the world of fairies. Lewis Carroll was deeply interested in occult phenomena: he had many books on this subject in his library, and was a founder member of the Society for Psychical Research, remaining a member until his death. This kind of interest was common in Victorian times, and prominent personalities from all walks of life were members of the SPR. Carroll went as far as to tabulate the incidence of psychic states in *Sylvie and Bruno*. George MacDonald, being a mystic, had little interest or need for the verification of psychic phenomena. However, he did attend lectures in Hastings given by a Polish mesmerist named Zamoiski, putting him into *David Elginbrod* (1863) as 'von Funkelstein'. His story *The Portent* (1860) featured as its heroine a girl named Alice (!) who was somnambulistic. (*The Portent* deals with the Highland belief in 'second sight'). That some of Carroll's knowledge of fairies came from a Scottish source is acknowledged in *Bruno's Revenge*:

> . . . What is the best time for seeing fairies? I believe I can tell you all about that. The first rule is, that it must be a *very* hot day – that we may consider as settled: and you must be just a *little* sleepy – but not too sleepy to keep your eyes open, mind. Well, you ought to feel a little – what one may call 'fairyish' – the Scotch call it 'eerie', and perhaps that's a prettier word; if you don't know what it means, I'm afraid I can hardly explain it; you must wait till you meet a fairy, and then you'll know.

Bruno's Revenge appeared in 1867, the same year as MacDonald's *Dealing with the Fairies*. Three of the five stories in that collection had already appeared in *Adela Cathcart* (1864). But Carroll had seen one of them, *The Light Princess*, as early as 1862. The surviving diaries resume on May 9, 1862: on July 9, Carroll wrote:

> To Tudor Lodge (Regent's Park) where I met Mr. MacDonald coming out. I walked a mile or so with him, on his way to a publisher with the MS of his fairy tale 'The Light Princess', in which he showed me some exquisite drawings by Hughes.

On May 9, 1863, Carroll noted:

> Heard from Mrs. MacDonald about 'Alice's Adventures Under Ground', which I had lent them to read, and which they wish me to publish.

Greville, then about 6, recalled that reading in his *Reminiscences* (p.15):

> I remember that first reading well, and also my braggart avowal that I wished there were 60,000 volumes of it.

There is some discrepancy here concerning the illustrations. Greville stated that the copy that his mother read to the family was illustrated by Carroll. Yet, according to Carroll's diaries, he did not complete the illustrations until Sept. 13, 1864. Possibly the illustrations were incomplete, assuming that Greville was correct in this detail.

There have been many who have claimed a share in bringing about the publication of the first *Alice* book. Yet the MacDonalds must be granted a foremost place. Indeed George MacDonald may even have influenced Carroll in his choice of Tenniel as illustrator. MacDonald's favourite fairy tale, as he tells us in his essay, *The Fantastic Imagination*, was Fouque's *Undine*. This story was published as part of a quartet, *The Four Seasons*, and reissued by Edward Lumley in 1861 with *Undine* illustrated by John Tenniel. And *The Four Seasons* was Carroll's original title for *Sylvie and Bruno*.

The Carroll/MacDonald friendship has even more significant ramifications when considered in relation to what each had written before they met. Prior to 1858, Carroll had published only a few poems and short stories in *The Whitby Gazette* (1854), *The Comic Times* (1855), and *The Train* (1856–7). The two anonymous poems which he claimed were published in *The Oxonian Advertiser* in 1854 are so undistinguished that they cannot be identified. In these early poems the chief influences are Tennyson and Thomas Hood.

George MacDonald also began his writing career as a poet, and produced most of his fairy tales for children at the time of his closest association with Carroll. (*Phantastes* was called by the author *A Faerie Romance for Men and Women*). It is therefore reasonable to conclude that these two writers, who shared a common – or rather uncommon – imagination, influenced each other, while retaining their own marked individuality of expression.

It was appropriate that in 1867, the year which saw the publication of

Dealings with the Fairies and *Bruno's Revenge*, MacDonald, in his essay *The Imagination*, (later collected in *Orts*, 1882), should pay a tribute to that quality in his friend. He was illustrating the point that 'the imagination often gets a glimpse of the law before it can be *ascertained* to be a law':

> ... a mathematical friend, a lecturer at one of the universities ... had lately *guessed* that a certain algebraic process could be shortened exceedingly if the method which his imagination suggested should prove to be a true one ... He put it to the test of experiment ... and found the method true. It has since been accepted by the Royal Society.

The work in question was the *Condensation of Determinants* (1866), published under the name of Dodgson.

III

STONES FROM BURIED TEMPLES

A comparison of the fairy tales of MacDonald and Carroll will reveal certain common elements of symbolism and association.

A collection of three of MacDonald's fairy tales, *The Wise Woman*, *The Carasoyn*, and *The Golden Key*, was published in the Ballantine series in 1972 under the collective title of *Evenor*. This was not MacDonald's title, but was taken by the editor, Lin Carter, from Plato – 'Evenor the Earth-Born', an Adamic figure. Lin Carter explains his choice:

> MacDonald sees terrestial nature as a maternal or paternal figure, and his stories, which contain numerous enigmatic and mysterious figures of divine authority, almost seem to share this element of Platonic mysticism. (p.xiv)

In fact, most of these figures were feminine, and an obvious symbol of Mother Nature. She appears very early in MacDonald's work, in the poem 'A Hidden Life' (1857), a quotation from which prefaces the Ballantine collection:

> ... Behind those world-enclosing hills
> There sat a mighty woman, with a face
> As calm as life, when its intensity
> Pushes it nigh to death ...

In Carroll's unpublished diaries, we find, opposite the entry for Jan. 9, 1855, the following extract from Shelley's 'Vision of Ocean':

> ... At the helm sits a woman more fair
> Than Heaven, when, unbinding its star-braided hair,
> It sinks with the sun on the earth and the sea.

She clasps a bright child on her up-gathered knee,
It laughs at the lightning, it mocks the mixed thunder
Of the air and the sea . . .

Could this be an anticipation of the motherly 'Sylvie' and 'the merry mocking Bruno'?

She appears as 'North Wind', as the 'Wise Woman', as the Grandmother in the *Princess* books, and – earliest of all in MacDonald's prose works – as the mysterious lady in the first chapter of *Phantastes*. She is the same figure as Mother Cary, in *The Water Babies*, and the Fairy Godmother, or Good Fairy, in fairy literature. But in MacDonald she is more personalised than in the works of other writers. She is, in fact, a symbol of Divinity in the feminine aspect, worshipped in ancient times as Isis, Aphrodite, and in many other forms, surviving today in the Madonna cult of the Mediterranean countries. In Carroll, she appears as 'Alice', who acts as a mother when the Duchess throws her baby to her, and 'Sylvie', who is more of a mother than sister to Bruno. Appropriately, 'Alice' was born on the Isis, as the Thames is known at Oxford.

So far, these personifications have been of the positive aspect – of love and goodness. But there is the other side of the coin – the negative aspect, of evil and destructiveness. These also we find in our authors, as the Alder-maiden in *Phantastes*, and in an exceptionally intense and savage form as *Lilith*, the very incarnation of evil. Many, including his son Greville, have claimed that *Lilith* (1895) was George MacDonald's greatest work. It is certainly his most disturbing book, and greatly upset Mrs. MacDonald. The author himself believed it was divinely inspired. Side-by-side with the allegory of a personal quest, is a theme few writers have ever tackled – the turning of a spirit that has pursued the path of evil to the path of atonement.

Carroll too was highly conscious of the problem of evil. He saw the very word as a reversal of 'live' (in *Sylvie and Bruno*). He was, as we know from the diaries and the introduction to *Pillow Problems*, constantly battling with the 'blasphemous thoughts' that assailed him. In *Alice*, it is the absence of love that causes the baby to change into a pig, and likewise Uggug, in *Sylvie and Bruno* becomes a porcupine (a prickly pig). The mothers here are negative 'Aphrodite' figures, as we may call them, reminding us of Circe, who changed the followers or Odysseus into swine, one of the 'totem' animals of ancient Aphrodite-worship.

Another of these figures, which appears early in Carroll's work, is the maiden in 'The Three Voices' (1855), who torments the care-free stroller on the beach into a state of gibbering insanity. But the best-known of these negative types are in the *Alice* books – the Duchess, the Queen of Hearts, the Red Queen. In *Alice on the Stage* (1887), Carroll wrote:

I pictured to myself the Queen of Hearts as a sort of embodiment of ungovernable passion – a blind and aimless Fury. The Red Queen I pictured as a Fury, but of another type; her passion must be cold and calm . . .

The Furies were the avenging deities of the Romans, but their origin is older: so terrible were they that people were afraid to call them by their real name.

In both MacDonald and Carroll, dream-states, and the transitions from dreaming to waking and vice versa, are central features, and are treated in a direct and natural way.

> ... I suddenly ... became aware of the sound of running water near me, and, looking out of bed, I saw that a large green marble basin, in which I was accustomed to wash, and which stood on a low pedestal of the same material in a corner of my room was overflowing like a spring; and that a stream of clear water was running over the carpet all the length of the room, finding its outlet I knew not where. And, stranger still, where this carpet, which I myself designed to imitate a field of grass and daisies, bordered the course of the little stream, the grassblades and daisies seemed to wave in a tiny breeze that followed the water's flow; while under the rivulet they bent and swayed with every motion of the changeful current, as if they were about to dissolve with it, and, forsaking their fixed form, become fluent as the waters.
>
> My dressing-table was an old-fashioned piece of furniture of black oak, with drawers all down the front. These were elaborately carved in foliage, of which ivy formed the chief part. The nearer end of this table remained just as it had been, but on the further end a singular change had commenced. I happened to fix my eye on a little cluster of ivy-leaves. The first of these was evidently the work of the carver; the next looked curious; the third was unmistakeable ivy; and just beyond it a tendril of clematis had twined itself about the gilt handle of one of the drawers. Hearing next a slight motion above me, I looked up, and saw that the branches and leaves designed upon the curtains of my bed were slightly in motion. Not knowing what change might follow next, I thought it high time to get up; and springing from the bed, my bare feet alighted upon a cool green sward; and although I dressed in all haste, I found myself completing my toilet under the boughs of a great tree ...   (*Phantastes*, ch.2)

In Carroll, these transitions are greatly condensed. 'Wool and Water' (ch.5 of *Through the Looking-Glass*) contains four such episodes. In the last, the Sheep places an egg that Alice has bought on a shelf at the end of the shop, for Alice to fetch ('I never put things into people's hands – that would never do – you must get it for yourself').

> 'I wonder *why* it wouldn't do?' thought Alice, as she groped her way among the tables and chairs, for the shop was very dark towards the end. 'The egg seems to get further away the more I walk towards it. Let me see, is this a chair? Why, it's got branches, I declare! How very odd to find trees growing here! And actually here's a little brook! Well, this is the very queerest shop I ever saw!'

So she went on, wondering more and more at every step, as everything turned into a tree the moment she came up to it, and she quite expected the egg to do the same. .... However, the egg only got larger and larger, and more and more human: when she had come within a few yards of it, she saw that it had eyes and a nose and mouth; and when she had come close to it, she saw clearly that it was HUMPTY DUMPTY himself.

The framework of *Through the Looking-Glass* is that of a game of Chess, with the looking-glass as the entrance to the dream world. But a new and disturbing element intrudes when Alice meets the sleeping Red King:

'He's dreaming now,' said Tweedledee: 'and what do you think he's dreaming about?'

Alice said 'Nobody can guess that.'

'Why, about *you*!' Tweedledee exclaimed, clapping his hands trium-phantly. 'And if he left off dreaming about you, where do you suppose you'd be?'

'Where I am now, of course,' said Alice.

'Not you!' Tweedledee retorted contemptuously. 'You'd be no-where. Why, you're only a sort of thing in his dream!' 'If that there King was to wake,' added Tweedledum, 'you'd go out – bang! – just like a candle!'

The problem continues to worry Alice, and at one stage she considers waking the Red King, to see what happens. The book ends with Alice dicussing the matter with the Black Kitten.

'Now, Kitty, let's consider who it was that dreamed it all. This is a serious question, my dear, and you should *not* go on licking your paw like that ... it *must* have been either me or the Red King. He was part of my dream, of course – but then I was part of his dream too! *Was* it the Red King Kitty? ..., *do* help to settle it! I'm sure your paw can wait!' But the provoking kitten only began on the other paw, and pretended it hadn't heard the question. Which do *you* think it was?

The terminal poem ends:

Life, what is it but a dream?

The prefatory poem to *Sylvie and Bruno* (1889) begins with the same question:

Is all our Life, then, but a dream?

In the *Sylvie and Bruno* books, instead of the story being one con-tinuous dream, there are constant alternations – sometimes very abrupt – between dreaming and waking. We are reminded of MacDonald's *At the Back of the North Wind*, in which the story also progresses by such alternations, though the transitions are not so sudden. (*At the Back of the*

North Wind was serialised in *Good Words for the Young*, 1868–70, before Carroll began expanding *Bruno's Revenge* into *Sylvie and Bruno*.)

There is, however, an important difference in the way MacDonald and Carroll treat the dreaming/waking sequences. With MacDonald, the dream is a way into the world of allegory. Carroll began by using the dream as a framework for 'nonsense', then became interested in the mechanics of the process, and in its metaphysical implications.

> '. . . either I've been dreaming about Sylvie,' I said to myself, 'and this is the reality. Or I've been with Sylvie, and this is the dream. Is Life itself a dream, I wonder?'   (*Sylvie and Bruno*, ch.2)

Others have, at various times in the past, been preoccupied with this problem. Martin Gardner, in his *The Annotated Alice* (1960) gives analogies with Bishop Berkeley and the Platonists. But there are even closer parallels, in the images and thoughts of the Taoist philosopher Chuang Tzu, who lived in China in the 3rd century BC:

> Once upon a time, I dreamed I was a butterfly, fluttering hither and thither. . . . Suddenly I woke up, and there I was, myself again. Now, I do not know whether I was then a man dreaming I was a butterfly, or whether I am now a butterfly dreaming I am a man . . .

(Compare this with MacDonald: 'It may be . . . that when most awake, I am only dreaming the more!' (*Lilith*, pp.350–51).)

A butterfly appears in *Through the Looking-Glass* (ch.3) – to be precise, a Bread-and-butter-fly – and could have appeared in ch.4, had not Tenniel preferred to illustrate a Carpenter instead, in the poem 'The Walrus and the Carpenter'. But to continue with Chuang Tzu:

> While they dream they do not know what they dream. Some will even interpret the very dream they are dreaming, and only when they awake do they know it was a dream . . . Fools think they are awake now, and flatter themselves they know if they are really princes or peasants. Confucius and you are both dreams, and I, who say you are dreams – I am but a dream myself –

which is precisely what the Tweedle brothers said to Alice.

The above was from ch.2 (of the first 33 'authentic' chapters, said to have been written by Chuang Tzu himself), called 'The Identity of Contraries'. In the first chapter, we encounter the legendary bird called the Rukh, an enormous creature whose wings obscure the sky – like those of the Monstrous Crow, whose shadow darkens and indeed ends the episode of the Red King's dream.

> One starts out for Yueh today and arrives there yesterday.

Reversals of time and direction occur in *Through the Looking-Glass* and *Sylvie and Bruno*.

It is easy to stop walking: the trouble is to walk without touching the ground.

The Red Queen manages this very well.

Is the blue of the sky its real colour, or the effect of distance?

asks Chuang Tzu.

What makes the sky such a darling blue?

asks Bruno (at the end of *Sylvie and Bruno Concluded.*)

I'm afraid he'll catch cold with lying of the damp grass,

said Alice of the Red King.

If you sleep on the damp ground you'll get lumbago,

says Chuang Tzu.

Did Carroll know the works of Chuang Tzu? They were first published in an English translation in 1881. In 1889, a translation by Herbert Giles appeared, with notes by Aubrey Moore, who was an Honorary Canon of Christ Church, Oxford. But also in Oxford was Dr. Legge, 'our Chinese Professor'. Thus, even if Carroll did not know of a published version, he could have learned of Chuang Tzu from others in his circle. We know, from an unpublished diary entry dated Nov. 24, 1857, that metaphysics was one of his subjects of special interest.

The first seven chapters of Chuang Tzu are traditionally called the 'inside' chapters, and the next fifteen the 'outside'. The meaning of these terms has been subject to dispute. But it is possible to accept them in the sense that MacDonald often uses them – as, for instance, in the title *Within and Without*, and in his fairy tales – a sense that is very much in the spirit of Chuang Tzu. If you are without, (i.e. *outside*) one world, you are *within* the other, and vice versa, and this can apply to the realms of matter and spirit. The meeting ground is the dream, where forms of our waking world mingle with those of the spirit world; Carroll called it 'Outland', in *Sylvie and Bruno* – an appropriate term, for it is outside our 'waking' world and Fairyland.

The idea of simultaneously-existing and interpenetrating worlds was also used by H. G. Wells (a letter from Wells to MacDonald pointing to similarities between *Lilith* (1895) and his novel *The Wonderful Visit*, published the same year, is given in the *Reminiscences*, pp.323–4). But it was used earlier. *Lilith* is prefaced by an extract from one of Thoreau's essays, 'Walking' (omitted from the Ballantine edition), which greatly influenced the early chapters of *Lilith*. Thoreau was an orientalist, and his writings and those of his friend Emerson are strongly Taoist in feeling.

Chuang Tzu was like Thoreau.

wrote Lin Yutang, in the introduction to his translation of Chuang Tzu (1948);

Emerson's two essays, 'Circles', and 'The Over-soul' are completely Taoist.

Emerson's poem 'The Mountain and the Squirrel' might have come straight out of Chuang Tzu. It was included, with four of her father's pieces, in Lilia MacDonald's anthology of poems for children, *Babies' Classics* (1904), completed by her sister Winifred following Lilia's early death.

Thoreau died in 1862, but both Carroll and MacDonald met Emerson in 1873.

The first *Sylvie and Bruno* book ends with a chapter entitled 'Looking Eastward', in which the words 'Look Eastward' are repeated many times. Carroll did travel eastward, in 1867, and got as far as Moscow. He invented a game for Alice Liddell which he called 'The Ural Mountains' – but she preferred him to continue the telling of *Alice's Adventures*. These were first written down when Carroll journeyed eastward, on the railway from Oxford to London. Martin Gardner has noted, in his *The Annotated Alice*, that in the Red King's dream,

the monarch is snoring on a square directly *east* of the square occupied by Alice.

And from *Phantastes* (ch. 7):

'In what direction are you going?' asked the old man.
'Eastward,' I replied.

This direction leads to China, the land of Chuang Tzu – another curious coincidence, perhaps best explained by Hubert Nicholson, in *A Voyage to Wonderland*:

It is safest to think of all these four books (the *Alices*, *Phantastes*, and *Lilith*) as having been built with stones fetched from the same ruined chapels and buried temples.   R.B.S.

Appendix C

TWO LETTERS FROM GEORGE MACDONALD TO PHOEBE POWELL

Phoebe Powell was a sister-in-law of George MacDonald. Greville MacDonald describes her as having 'a genius for philanthropy' (*Life*, p.101). She was also 'the best water-colour painter of them all' (ibid.). The first letter dates from the time of the composition of the first draft of 'Within and Without' (q.v. 1855): it must have been written very soon after his arrival at Newport, Isle of Wight. The second was written during the period of his incumbency as Congregationalist minister at Arundel, Sussex.

Newport, Dec. 10, 1850.

My dear Phoebe

This evening I have received your very kind note, for which accept my best thanks. I am sure if I am not blest, it will not be for want of good wishes from my dear friends. Thank you for your kind inquiries and remembrances. I hope my eyes *are* open, as you say, to see something of the many blessings that surround me – but sure I am that around me and around us all, there are thousands of blessings, which too much care prevents us from seeing, and yet of which we partake insensibly almost, as the flowers are cooled by the night-dew, and the limbs are refreshed by sleep. As we become more child-like towards God, we shall see these more clearly, and partake of their blessing more largely.

Surely I need not say that I did not leave mentioning your gift till now, because I had forgot it – indeed I did so because I wished to notice it by itself. Thank you many times for it, and for the kindness that made you send it. I like it very much, and hope yet to see it framed in my study, if I live to have one. You know I am not a judge, but I know that it wakes pleasurable feelings in me, and I presume that is all you expected from my ignorance when you so kindly sent it. I think I am better, but I dont get strong very fast. I should like better to be under homoeopathic treatment. I hope you are keeping pretty well, and not needing to use the

129

globules very often. There is no homoeopath here – but the system is making way amongst the people.

Believe me, my dear Phoebe,
  your very affectionate brother,
   George MacDonald

           Arundel, Oct. 17, 1851.

My dear Phoebe,

I fear you will think me very ungrateful that I have so long delayed writing to you. I did not mean to let one post pass without thanking you for the pretty drawing – *pretty* is not the word – which you have been so kind as to do for me. Indeed I value it very much, and the next thing I mean to get beyond [necessity?] is a frame for it, that I may hang it up in my study. How would it do to have a double frame, & put the Rydal lake alongside of it? But I think that will only do for works in the same style.

I was very busy last week, & you know when you do not do a thing immediately, how easily day after day slips away and yet it is not done. I will not try to excuse myself though.

How your mind must now be filled with new pictures and images. I enjoyed some of your accounts much. They will remain with you for ever, and will not merely affect every future drawing you employ yourself upon, but the effect on your mind will never pass away. Our country here is very different, yet very enjoyable – and the trees are now putting on the richer autumn tints, and prophesying of the spring. I always feel an exhilarating effect in the cold air of the autumn, but it soon changes into the biting of the frosty file-edged winter atmosphere which I am now expecting. Yet I think the leaves will last till Nov. when I expect a visit from Greville. He has great delight in colours, and I hope he will be able to see the colours in our woods. Despite what the mesmerisée said, I do think my *chief* delight is in form.

I am rather pleased that I have not to preach next Sunday – we have missionary sermons then. I think this is the first Sunday I have not preached since the ninth of March. I should have been very pleased if I could have run up to London & preached there, & seen you all. I heard your accounts of your journey, particularly some comments on your drawing of Wordworth's house. Many thanks to you my dear Phoebe – with love to Charlotte & Flora, & you too I am

    your loving brother
     George MacDonald

Appendix D

LETTER FROM ALEXANDER STRAHAN TO GEORGE MACDONALD

CONCERNING 'GUTTA-PERCHA WILLIE' (1873)

A transcript follows this facsimile: the first page is missing.

portion, and if we could get this on the 17th ins^t it would be in time for all purposes, and we should be grateful accordingly

Most sincerely yours

A Strahan

P.S. When speaking of money I forgot to mention the book "Gutta Percha Willie." It stands in this way:— I paid you £50 on account of it, and I paid for Mr Hughes's illustrations £94. 10/- (ninety guineas). One half of the latter sum is charged against the magazine, and the other against the book, £50, and £47. 5/-, in all £97. 5/-, have thus been paid out by me on account of the book. If you might to arrange directly with Mr King for the copyright of course you can do so (crediting me with the amount expended by me as above)) or (I shall arrange with Mr King, if you prefer it and credit you with all he may pay in excess of the above £97. 6/.

Transcript of final section of letter from Alexander Strahan to George MacDonald, *c.*1873, pp.3 on single folded sheet, the 4th page blank, with printed heading '12, Paternoster Row, E.C, London ——18—'.

'. . . portion, and if we could get this on the 17th inst, it would be in time for all purposes, and we should be grateful accordingly.
Most sincerely yours,
A. Strahan

PS. When speaking of money I forgot to mention the book "Gutta Percha Willie". It stands in this way:– I paid you £50 on account of it, and I paid for Mr. Hughes's illustrations £94.10/- (ninety guineas). One half of the latter sum is charged against the magazine, and the other against the book. £50 and £47.5/, in all £97.5/. have thus been paid out by me on account of the book. If you wish to arrange directly with Mr. King for the copyright of course you can do so (crediting me with the amount expended by me as above) or I shall arrange it with Mr. King, if you prefer it, and credit you with all he may pay in excess of the above £97.5/.
AS'

'The History of Gutta-Percha Willie' appeared in Strahan's *Good Words for the Young* in 1872. It was published in book form in 1873 by Henry S. King as *Gutta-Percha Willie, the Working Genius*.

LETTER FROM GEORGE MACDONALD TO HIS COUSIN JAMES MACDONALD

(reproduced from a poor original)

James MacDonald was then living at The Farm, Huntly, where George MacDonald had lived as a child. The 'meal' is oatmeal. The 'next story' is almost certainly 'What's Mine's Mine', 1886. The term 'occasional acting' is something of an understatement, and refers to the many performances the MacDonald family gave of Bunyan's *The Pilgrim's Progress*, Part II, between 1877 and 1887. The adaptation was made by Mrs. MacDonald and published by the Oxford University Press in 1925. George MacDonald played the part of Greatheart.

BORDIGHERA, MARCH 28, 1886.

MY VERY DEAR COUSIN;

I THANK YOU HEARTILY FOR YOUR KIND
LETTERS, AND FOR THE NEWSPAPER WITH THE REPORT OF YOUR LECTURE,
WHICH I NEED HARDLY SAY I READ WITH INTEREST--THOUGH I SHOULD HAVE
LIKED MUCH BETTER TO HEAR YOU GIVE IT. THE MEAL IS AT GENOA, WHERE
IT HAS BEEN FOR A WEEK BEFORE THEY LET ME KNOW IT HAD ARRIVED.
I SUSPECT IT IS NOBODY'S BUSINESS, AND SO HE DOES IT! I ENCLOSE A
CHEQUE FOR THE CARRIAGE WITH REAL GRATITUDE.

YOU HAVE A WRONG NOTION OF THE RELATION OF MY LIFE AND WORK TO
MY OCCASIONAL ACTING. IN THE FIRST PLACE, IT HAS BEEN A WELCOME REST
FROM THE MUCH HARDER LABOUR OF WRITING. IN THE NEXT, SEEING YOU
REGARD IT AS INTERFERING WITH MY WORK--IS NOT FORTY TWO BOOKS, ALL
TOLD, ENOUGH TO HAVE WRITTEN IN THIRTY YEARS? THEN ONCE MORE, I
LOOK UPON THE ART OF ACTING AS A VERY~~XXXXXXXXX~~ HIGH ONE; AND WHEN
I TELL YOU THAT BOTH BURNE JONES AND ROBERT BROWNING HAVE SPOKEN
OF OUR, OR RATHER OF MY WIFE'S WORK, FOR THE ARRANGEMENT IS ENTIRE-
LY HERS, AS AS NEAR PERFECTION AS THEY COULD WISH, YOU WILL NOT
THINK THAT WE HAVE ANY DOUBT ABOUT THE DIGNITY OF THE ENDEAVOUR.
I HAVE BEEN LAID UP, ALMOST FOR THE FIRST TIME THIS WINTER, OR
I WOULD HAVE WRITTEN TO YOU SOONER. WE HAVE HAD A SEVERE WINTER
FOR US, AS EVERYBODY ELSE HAS HAD. I SUPPOSE WEATHER DOES GO IN
CYCLES, ELSE WE SHOULD BE COMPELLED TO SAY THAT FINE WEATHER IS
GRADUALLY DEPARTING FROM THE EARTH.

I SHALL HAVE MY NEXT STORY OUT VERY SOON NOW. IT IS OUT OF MY
HANDS. I THINK YOU WILL SEE SOME OF THE SIGNS OF OUR LITTLE TALK
ABOUT SUTHERLAND-SHIRE IN IT.

I WONDER WHAT YOU THINK ABOUT IRELAND! I HAVE BEEN LONG OF THE
GROWING OPINION THAT NOTHING ELSE WILL DO BUT RE-CONQUEST, AND ~~PRE-~~
FRESH CONSTITUTION; AND TOWARDS THAT THINGS SEEM TO BE TENDING.
BUT THEY HAVE FROM THE FIRST BEEN USED ABOMINABLY, AND I CONFESS
TO A GREAT SYMPATHY WITH THE MALCONTENTS. THEY DO WELL TO BE ANGRY,
BUT VERY ILL TO BE ANGRY AFTER SUCH MEAN & CRUEL & UNJUST FASHION.
OF COURSE I WOULD HAVE THE GOVERNMENT WAIT FOR SUCH PROVOCATION--S
SURE TO COME--AS WOULD RENDER IT IMPERATIVE FOR SELF-PRESERVATION.
I HOPE THINGS ARE LOOKING A LITTLE BETTER WITH YOU.
WINNA 'T BE GRAN' WHAN A' THIS IS OWER, AN' WE'RE WI' THE AULD
FOWK AGAIN? MAN, I EXPEC' AWFU'!

YOURS LOVINGLY,

George MacDonald

CENTENARY OF BIRTH, 1924

The centenary of George MacDonald's birth witnessed the reissuing of *The Tragedie of Hamlet, Lilith, Fairy Tales* (the Fifield edition of 1904) and *The Diary of an Old Soul*. All were published by George Allen & Unwin, who also brought out Greville MacDonald's *George MacDonald and his Wife* in the same year.

Programme of Conversazione, held on the anniversary day, Dec. 10, at the Suffolk Galleries, Pall Mall, 8–11 p.m.

A copy of *The Portent and other stories* was presented to each guest (q.v. *The Portent*, 1864). The printed programme, 4to, pp.[4], has a photograph of George MacDonald on the cover, and decorated borders on the first three pages. The chairman was G. K. Chesterton, the vice-chairman Sir Johnston Forbes-Robertson. The proceedings consisted of speeches, vocal settings of six of MacDonald's poems, and recitations by Sir Johnston Forbes-Robertson and Bernard MacDonald, a son of the author. There was also an exhibition of items relating to the author's life and work – the only occasion, to date, that such an exhibition has been held. The printed programme is itself a scarce item: unfortunately a catalogue of the exhibition was not issued.

An appreciation by Harold Child appeared in *The Times*, Dec. 10, 1924. He also reviewed *George MacDonald and his Wife*, *Lilith* and *Fairy Tales*, in *The Times Literary Supplement*, May 29, 1924, in which the fairy stories are regarded as MacDonald's greatest achievement.

Notes on the boyhood of George MacDonald by Sir Edward Troup. *Aberdeen Press and Journal*, June 9, 1924. Sir Edward married MacDonald's fifth daughter Winifred in 1897.

Programme

*

Chairman	G. K. CHESTERTON
Vice-Chairman	Sir JOHNSTON FORBES-ROBERTSON

Speeches will be interspersed between items of the Programme, the order of which is subject to alteration.

1. The CHAIRMAN will speak

2. Miss ELSIE NICHOLL will sing
   Oh! The Bonnie, Bonnie Dell   Music by Minette

3. Sir JOHNSTON FORBES-ROBERTSON will read
   Sir Aglovaile through the Churchyard rode

4. Miss DOROTHEA WEBB will sing
   (a) *My Child*   Music by C. A. Macirone
   (b) *Baby*   „ „ Albert Mallinson
   (c) *A Christmas Carol* „ „ C. A. Macirone

5. Guests will join in a
   Thanksgiving Song (*vide* opposite)

6. Refreshments

7. Mr. BERNARD MacDONALD will recite
   No End to No-Story

8. Miss ELSIE NICHOLL will sing
   The Auld Fisher   Music by William Nicholl

*

The Reading, Recitation and Songs are all by George MacDonald.

Miss ELLA IVIMEY will be the Accompanist.

Exhibition of Items connected with George MacDonald's Life and Work.

Presentation to Guests of Commemorative Volume.

17.   Programme of the centenary of birth celebration of GMD held in London in 1924.

Appendix G

'AN INVALID'S WINTER IN ALGERIA'

The MacDonalds spent the winter of 1856–7 in Algiers at the suggestion of Lady Byron who also financed the trip (Life, pp.266–73). She had still not met George MacDonald at this period, but had been much impressed by Within and Without *(1855) and hoped the visit would prove beneficial to his health. The following article appeared in* Good Words, *1864, pp.793–9, and is here reprinted for the first time. The vivid impression of the rainbow (p.795) could well have influenced MacDonald's fairy tale 'The Golden Key' (1867).*

Waking, as I supposed, from one of those short troubled sleeps which chequer the monotony of the less violent forms of sea-sickness, I heard, to my great delight, the bell at the wheel announce a far more advanced hour of the morning than I could have hoped. Already the cool light was penetrating the thick glass in the porthole of my cabin. I rose, and slowly crept on deck. It was as if the bitterness of death were past, and I had awaked in the new world. From the narrow grave of my berth, filled with a close atmosphere and haunted by unpleasant noises and motions, I came forth in the midst of the wide sea and sky. Through the crowds of French soldiers and other passengers, I elbowed my way to the wheel, and there finding an open space, I looked around me. Speedily sped the vessel southwards, away from the cold winds and frosts of a northern winter, whose advanced guard had overtaken us on our way, and kept us for days imprisoned. But now we had escaped. And the sun would soon rise, and by the time he should have reached the zenith we hoped to be at anchor in the port of Algiers. This morning was a new vision to me. Over us hung, or rather stooped, the sky of the south, a deep violet, with much of the red in it; wherein the stars sparkled with a keen steely lustre, like spangles cut from sword-blades. Underneath flowed the sea, with great dashes of purple upon a slate-blue, that swept and rolled and floated away to the east, where the sky-sea, barred with orange and yellow, told that the sun was near. Two or three sea-birds were following close behind us; and suddenly through the waves came a troop of porpoises,

This, all but illimitable, expansion of our knowledge of countries far and near, has a meaning, the import of which it would not be easy duly to appreciate. It has two meanings—first, it *signifies the fact* that the English race has spread itself abroad in a manner, and to an extent, that has no parallel in the history of nations. Its second meaning is prospective chiefly, and it foreshows what is the destiny of this race, and of this language, and of this Anglo-Saxon feeling—this constitutional organisation—

this home-habit, and this Christianity. We have come to know distant lands thus intimately, *for a reason*, namely, this—that we are preparing to send thither, and we are now actually sending thither, our sons and daughters, and brothers and sisters. Within the compass of another thirty years from this time, if Europe be left to its dozen of nationalities, the five continents, or four of them, will be teeming with the English people, and will be vivified by English institutions.

AN INVALID'S WINTER IN ALGERIA.

ALGIERS.

WAKING, as I supposed, from one of those short troubled sleeps which chequer the monotony of the less violent forms of sea-sickness, I heard, to my great delight, the bell at the wheel announce a far more advanced hour of the morning than I could have hoped. Already the cool light was penetrating the thick glass in the porthole of my cabin. I rose, and slowly crept on deck. It was as if the bitterness of death were past, and I had awaked in the new world. From the narrow grave of my berth, filled with a close atmosphere and haunted by unpleasant noises and motions, I came forth in the midst of the wide sea and sky. Through the crowds of French soldiers and other passengers, I elbowed my way to the wheel, and there finding an open space, I looked around me. Speedily sped the vessel southwards, away from the cold winds and frosts of a northern winter, whose advanced guard had overtaken us on our way, and kept us for days imprisoned. But now we had escaped. And the sun would soon rise, and by the time he should have reached the zenith we hoped to be at anchor in the port of Algiers. This morning was a new vision to me. Over us hung, or rather stooped, the sky of the south, a deep violet, with much of the red in it; wherein the stars sparkled with a keen steely lustre, like spangles cut from sword-blades. Underneath flowed the sea, with great dashes of purple upon a slate-blue, that swept and rolled and floated away to the east, where the sky-sea, barred with orange and yellow, told that the sun was near. Two or three sea-birds were following close behind us; and suddenly through the waves came a troop of porpoises, rushing along with

18.   First page of an article by GMD appearing in *Good Words* (1864) not previously recorded.

rushing along with wondrous speed; shooting out of one wave, and plunging headlong into the next; gambolling, and coursing, and bounding, as if trying their *wind* against the steamer, and easily able to pass her if they chose. I thought what a delicious life they had of it in the waves, with their cool slippery sides, that were always wet; and how they felt as much at home in the water as we in the air, knowing it was their only element. And then I began to pity them that they had only the Mediterranean to swim in, and were so unlikely ever to find the way out into the great world-sea. But I knew that this was only the longing for freedom in me, which can never be stilled by limitless room, but must find the boundless in another region than that of space and time.

At length the hills arose and drew near. Ere long we saw the white city built up the face of one of the low range – the Sahel that guards the coast; from the summits of which the pirates used to search the face of the sea for the white-winged game, that so often fled in vain before the swift hunters of the waves. Soon we were in the midst of swarthy visages and glowing eyes, that might well belong to the descendants of those terrible men; and ere long, we were guided by one of them to a hotel in the principal *place* of the town, where, by-and-by, we contrived to forget the horrors of the steamer in the less, but not less real, horrors which mingle with the comforts of a French hotel.

It was the end of November; yet, invalid as I was, I dressed next morning with the window open. The day was so glowing, the air so clear, and the colours of sea and earth and sky were so intense, that the whole scene looked like one of those pictures one does not believe in. Across the still, blue bay, we saw the purple hills which continue the range on which the city is built; and beyond them rose in the distance blue mountains with snowy summits, around which we could see the tops of lower hills crouching like lions at their feet. Above all spread the cloudless blue. The square on which my window looked, and which, open on one side, revealed the scene of which I write, was crowded with a bewildering variety of the most brilliant costumes. The splendid dresses of Moors and Jews mingled with the numberless varieties of the uniforms of French soldiers; while the rainbow mass was relieved by the graceful simplicity of the Arab bernouse, and the mournful white of the shrouded Moorish women, who seemed already half buried from life and clothed in the garments of the grave – where, even if the spirit lingered by the mouldering form, they could scarce feel less lonely and hopeless than they at least appear to the eyes of the English stranger. The whole was filled with military noises, in which the kettle-drum, with its terrier-like alarum, took a foremost part, and soon wearied us with its regularly recurring noisy monotony. Indeed, we were very soon sick of the tumult, indoors and out, and longed for the seclusion of the country.

From the sea, the outline of the city, lying on the slope of the hill, somewhat resembles in form one of the Moorish horseshoe arches, but bent outwards considerably at the heel – expanding, that is, when it reaches the more level ground at the base of the hill. The whole mass is of a dazzling whiteness, resembling the escarpment of a chalk hill; for twice a year they whitewash the whole of their houses outside and inside, to protect themselves from the heat, though thereby they expose themselves the more to the injurious effects of the light. Some of the principal streets, where the mortifying hand of the conquerors has been at work, are entirely French in their appearance; but as soon as you turn southwards, and commence to climb one of the streets which lead up the hill, you find yourself in an entirely novel environment; wandering in the labyrinth of an apparently endless accumulation of narrow streets, and stairs, and passages, and archways, shooting off in all directions; some ascending towards the sunlight as you hope, others appearing to dive into the earth; all narrow, many so narrow that a little person could easily touch both sides at once; many arched over, and many roofed in by the contact of the projecting upper stories of the houses on opposite sides. The design is to exclude the sun in all ways. The rubbish can only be removed on the backs of donkeys, of which you may often meet a troop in your way emerging from what seems the entrance to a splendid mansion, or jolting along a squalid lane three or four feet wide. But, although the streets are so narrow, it must not be supposed that the town is therefore as ill-aired as, with such appearances, an English one would be justly supposed to be: for inside every house – whose heavy door looks like that of a prison – in these narrow passages is a square court open to the heavens, so that 'each has its own patch of sky, and little lot of stars.' Along these streets I much enjoyed wandering. Some of them are full of workshops (little rooms, or scarcely more than closets) open to the street, above which they are sometimes raised a few feet. In these the various trades go on – tailoring, shoemaking, turning, tobacco-cutting, and others. Conversations might easily be carried on across the streets between the different artisans. I used sometimes to stand and watch them at their work, and generally saw something to interest me. One time it was the extraordinary development and use of the great toe, supplying the place of a thumb on the turning-lathe – one hand being employed to turn the lathe with a bow, while the operator sat on the floor on a level with his machine. Another time it was the covering of a button with a network of silk; or a stitch new to me in shoemaking; or the moulding of red clay-pipes; or the scraping of the shell of a clumsy musical instrument, which looked like a dropsical guitar. But I had not much opportunity for making acquaintance with these streets; for, after many failures, we at length succeeded in finding an *appartement* in a large Moorish house, belonging to a French officer, at the distance of two miles from the city; and here we settled down for the winter, exulting in the hope of privacy and leisure, with an open silence all around us, wherein the soul might feel that the whole external world is (as Schleiermacher says) the extension of the human body, and might flow forth and occupy its dwelling without hindrance from contact with uncongenial forms. The room in which we sat had a low groined roof, with vaulted recesses on one side, in which we soon contrived to put a

French piano, and on a cheffonier in the other a statuette of the Venus of Milo; finding thus some relief to the picturesque dulness of the room. The floor was paved with coloured tiles, rising a couple of feet up the walls; but the entire absence of red in any combination prevented these tiles from continuing to please me much. Then the room was disfigured by a huge French stove in one of the small windows, which, when it became necessary to use it, added much to our discomfort by smoking. But through our little windows we saw the Mediterranean at a furlong's distance; and when its sunny face drew us out to the little terrace at the top of the entrance-stair, we were in the midst of a glowing world; the great hills in the distance, like an infinite hope, and the air filled with the odours of citron and orange-blossoms. Here our days passed quietly. For some time the weather was warm enough to sit reading out of doors upon the rocky cliffs by the tideless sea; on which, when you looked up from your book, you might see the boats of the country, with their elegant three-cornered latteen sails on the long slanting yard, bounding before a breeze from the west, when the white water is coming out of the black, as my little girl said. Or in one of those cloudy days, which were comparatively rare there, you might see these boats dreaming along over a floor of delicate silver-grey, turning up ever as they broke the surface, and leaving behind them a track of brilliant intense blue, corresponding to a belt of the same colour that circled the edge of the far horizon. Or, if the sun had gone behind the hills, and sea and sky built up one cavern of calm blue, you might catch the rosy glow of a single sail, which alone, in the midst of the prevailing blue, reflected the sunset red. But over all, I think the colours of this new land affected me most. Yet there were no gorgeous sunsets, such as in our England, to crown earthly vapours with unearthly glory. The sky was too clear for those. The hills lying immediately behind us prevented our seeing the actual sunset, whereof the only noticeable sign in middle air might be a pale pink vapour, in the centre of which might sparkle one diamond star. Nor was there any common-grass – no fields with thick carpets of grass, wherein even the foot has its own sensuous joy, and whereon you may cast yourself down in silence when the love of the earth becomes too strong for happiness. Only once did the feeling of earth's homeliness enter my soul. It was an early spring night. A heavy dew falls at sundown, but after that it is often warm and dry. We had just left the house of some Scotch friends, who, like ourselves, had spent the winter there, and who long ere this had become dear to us. It was a night of stars. Venus was going down in the west in a triumph of glory, flashing red, and green, and blue, like a sea-beacon, through the refracting strata of the lower atmosphere. The whole night-vault was filled with the roarings of the waves which a wind, since dead, had aroused, and driven landward to rave on the rocky shore. And suddenly to my soul came a scent of earth, of damp spring earth, an odour well known from childhood, which calls up thoughts of love and the grave, and mingles with either kind, for they are not far apart. Then I recognised the common mother – knew that England and

Africa were of the same earth, and rejoiced that she bore me.

But with the new year a stormy time began. For many, many weeks there was more or less rain every day, sometimes, but rarely, continuous for two or three days, accompanied by violent storms of wind and lightning. Then we could go out but little. We read, or sat and gazed through our tiny windows on the turmoil of the sea. Far out from the shore reached the white chaos of the breakers. In mingling shades of green, and yellow, and white, barred and patched with the purple shadows of the clouds, the sea tossed and foamed beneath the wind, which tore the glassy tops of the billows into hair-like spray. During this season you might sometimes see fine masses of cloud, but seldom such as, during thunderous weather, may be seen, like grotesque masses of half-finished sculpture, piled in Titanic confusion and magnificence around our sky. The rain falls like a cataract. Once I saw the finest rainbow I have ever seen. It planted one end of its arch close beside us, between us and the sea, and rose aloft and stretched away the other where we could not see it for the heights around us. I never saw one come so near. It would have been easy to find the golden key at its foot this time. But what struck me most was the intensity of its chords of thick colour. A second larger arc appeared beyond it; but its root was planted far out in the sea, and its hues were thin, and vague, and ghostly beside the glow of the nearer.

With the night came often the lightning and the thunder. It was so dark without, that to us looking from within the windows appeared solid as the walls, when suddenly a sea and sky immense asserted themselves with an instantaneous illumination of existence in the soul, flashing themselves in through the narrow windows – for a small opening admits a great space; then darkness followed, rent and billowed by the thunder. Such a stormy winter had not been known by any of the French inhabitants.

Now and then I took a few hours' ride in the surrounding country, among the low hills which crowd the coast. As there are but few large trees, and at this season little vegetation, the country has in many parts rather a bare look, but in the gorges between the hills there are many bushes and small trees. The most striking plants are the prickly-pear cactus and the aloe. This cactus forms a defence around and throughout the Arab villages. But what seemed to interest me most was the Arab cemeteries. One of the largest of these lay on the top and seaward slope of a hill, from which the inhabitants of the near village, a noted nest of pirates, used to search the sea for their prey. Of this village only miserable huts remain amidst the ruins of Moorish houses. The number-less graves with their tiny vertical stones lie broad and bare to the sea and the sky; unlike the greater number of their churchyards, which lie in groves of olive and other trees. Suddenly, when riding along a narrow bridlepath, you find yourself in the midst of one of these chambers of the dead; and looking back you see, perhaps, that for some little way you have been riding through graves, crowded among the roots of the trees.

Over the resting-places of their chief men they build small mosques, or, in some cases, mere low-roofed huts, but better than many of the dwellings of the living. I entered one of these, and found the floor filled with tombs, one apparently very old; and one or two in the usual form of the more elaborate tombs of the country, with a high ornamented stone at the head and feet, connected by two long side-stones, across which were little shelves with hollows for water, and I think flowers. Some earthen lamps stood on the old tomb; and babies' graves were near the door. It was a solemn place. The light through the rents in the walls or roof fell in faint brown patches on the earthen floor. This, and that which entered by the low ever-open door, was the sole sombre illumination of the place, which had a cathedral stillness and sacredness about it, mingled with that feeling of faint desolation which in every land and under every form the forsaken graves of men and women awake in the heart.

But oftener I went into the city, never tired of looking at the varied human forms that met me on my way. One cannot help wondering, when he sees the the little, jerky, self-asserting, tight-laced Frenchman beside the stately, dignified, reserved, loose-robed Arab, how the former could ever assume and retain authority over the latter. I have seen a power of contempt and repressed indignation in the half-sidelong look with which an Arab in a ragged bernouse regarded a Frenchman, who had tapped him on the shoulder with a stick to attract his attention. There is something in the bearing and manners of the Arab significant, whether truly or not, of a personal dignity far beyond that common to the German, or French, or English. Two of them came once to our residence to remove our piano before we left. A great proportion of the heavy carriage in Algiers is done by the Arabs slinging the weight on a pole which rests on their shoulders. Our breakfast being still on the table, I asked them to sit down and have some coffee; which they did without the least embarrassment, half-lounging on their chairs, and chatting away in bad French, aided by gesture, with a thoroughbred ease rarely to be seen in our own country. I was proud of them. Their religion teaches them that in the sight of God they are all equal, and they seem to believe it, more at least than Christians do; and this, combined with their fatalism, which naturally destroys all haste and perturbation, produces an indifferent stateliness of demeanour which many a man of Norman blood and fabulous origin might well envy. One or two of them, whom I came to know a little, used always to shake hands with me after the English fashion. Indeed, they seem to like the English much: *Inglese bono* are frequently the first words you hear from their lips. Some English ladies we know had favour shown them to the degree of being permitted to enter the mosques without putting off their shoes, being only required to wipe them very carefully on a mat brought them for the purpose. I was amused at being recognised in the streets as an Englishman, because I was partly dressed in the Highland costume. But, indeed, the Highlander is the type of the English soldier with them. This notion the native African troops have brought back with them from the Crimea. Once I was standing in the principal market-place, when one of a little group of French and Maltese about me touched me and pointed to the sign of a *cabaret* opposite, upon which appeared a Highlander and a Zouave fraternising hand-in-hand. They seemed desirous I should acknowledge the relationship.

There are many negroes amongst the inhabitants of Algiers – the young remarkable, if rarely for beauty of features, yet often for the fine formation of the limbs, and for delicacy in the texture of the skin. The old, on the contrary, both in feature and limb, are something frightful. I feel almost guilty of inhumanity in writing it; yet so they affected me. Some of the Jews likewise present as exaggerated forms of the features peculiar to their race as caricature could desire; while the Jewesses are almost invariably unpleasant-looking. In Tangiers, on the contrary, where there is a mixture of Spanish blood in the race, the Jews are, I am informed, a very fine people. But in Algiers, from being constantly treated with all the distinctions of a separate and inferior race, they seem to have degenerated. To return to the negroes. From the fact that the Moors do not permit their young women to go to the mosque, and, therefore, that their religious necessities are left unsupplied, some of the negresses have attained great influence over the Moorish women; seeming, indeed, to occupy the position of priestesses between them and some good or bad power which they attempt either to propitiate or disarm by barbarous ceremonies. At certain wells on the coast negresses meet one day in every week, to sacrifice fowls and perform other rites. To these assemblies some of the Moorish women repair, to have their faces laved in the holy water, and be fumigated by the negresses with incense. But on frequent occasions they assemble in an appointed house – that is, in the central open court of one of the Moorish dwellings, and anyone may easily gain admittance. At one of these I was present, but I should not choose to go again; it left such an impression of doleful, uninteresting horror. Nor were the performances at all such as to be worth describing. They consisted chiefly of intense bewildering noise from half-a-dozen drums, as many iron castanets, and some other instruments, accompanied at times with a most peculiar shrill whistle, resembling that of a steam-engine, from one or other of the negresses, with which they used to excite others to join in the second principal part of the performance – namely, a kind of frantic and degrading dance, in which at one time they threw themselves heels over head on the ground, and at another crawled backwards, beating time with their hands on the paved floor; or, again, belaboured themselves with ropes, and pretended to stab themselves with knives. Whenever anyone seemed going too far, or likely to injure himself, another patted him on the back, and at once brought him to his senses. At length, however, one or two were carried away senseless. This kind of performance, I understand, is usually kept up to a late hour; and in many cases, when the excitement reaches its height, marvellous tricks of jugglery are said to be performed, though I witnessed none of these myself that were at all wonderful. But the solemnity of the countenances of the performers, and the appearance of earnestness in their work, while it had something ludicrous in it, I yet found impressive and affecting. May it not be, I thought, that even in this there are the first rudiments of the expression of an unknown need? – an inward prayer, that is yet so undefined as to take no embodiment in articulate sound, but utters itself in howls and artificial noises? These too are the children of the one Father, and there may be even in these orgies something of prayer that reaches the ear that listens not for the form of the words, but the utterance of the need. And I could not help collating these barbarities with some forms of Christian worship, good enough in themselves, but which, when exalted into the place of essential duty, seemed to me equally senseless with these half-animal utterances, and far more provoking, as being forced on the attention by persons whose appearance and development in other things seem to justify the expectation of something much further beyond their negro brothers and sisters. At these exhibitions many Moorish women are present, but they take no other share in the performances than receiving every now and then what seems a benediction, in the form of being twisted by the shoulders from one side to the other and back, accompanied by other manipulations from the negresses; and inhaling now and then the odours of the fumigations proceeding from an earthen sherd with live charcoal, on which incense is sprinkled, and held under their faces.

Very different in purport and effect is the worship of the Mohamme-dans, to whom, however, the negroes belong, at least in name, although the remnants of old superstitions yet retain a power over them. One fine moonlight night, during the Fast of Ramadan, my wife and I set out to walk to the town, that we might see the principal mosque lighted up for worship. Such good order is preserved under the rule of the French, and such is the quiet behaviour of the inhabitants generally, that we were far safer in doing so than we should have been in the neighbourhood of any large town in our own country. The streets were beginning to be deserted as we went through. After passing along a blank wall, within a colonnade in one of the principal streets, for some distance, a gloomy-looking door in it, on being pushed open, admitted us into a kind of piazza, which ran round three sides of an open court. In this passage a fountain stood for the frequent washing enjoined by their law. The fourth side of the quadrangle was formed by the open arches of the roofed part of the mosque, which inner part seemed a much larger quadrangle than the outer, and was all divided into small square portions, by lines of pillars and arches intersecting each other at right angles. The arches running in one direction were all plain, those crossing them ornamented by having the underside cut into many little arches. Along every avenue of pillars, running from the entrance inwards, was suspended a row of oil-lamps, consisting of glass basins with floating wicks. These rows, when approaching the opposite wall began to ascend, and the lamps were carried gradually up the wall a short way, so as to give the appearance of a long perspective of lights. There were very few worshippers present, and these scattered in little groups throughout the building, but mostly at the upper end, where we heard the low tones of the priest's voice, in listening to which the worshippers now stood, now kneeled, and now bowed low with their foreheads to the ground. Once or twice a Moor, who seemed to have some charge in the observances, waived us away with dignity when he saw us; but we moved to a different part of the building, and had no other interruption to our curiosity. But the most picturesque point of view was the exterior court. Here the moon shone clear into the court, here light falling upon a large tree in the centre, around which clung the stem of a great vine. As we looked up we saw one of the towers of the mosque rising high above us into the night, with the faint glimmer of the moonlight on the glazed tiles which ornamented it near the top, around which was disposed a coronal of dull lamps, like those in the mosque below, and which showed reddish in the pale moonshine. Then on the other side opened the wide, strong arches, with the long rows of lamps stretching far into the distance of the mosque.

Stormy as the season was, the common red geranium had been in blossom in the hedges all the winter through. We had never been quite without flowers; but now, as the spring came on, the new children of the year began to arrive. I am no botanist, and my knowledge of the flowers is like my knowledge of the human kind. I have a few friends, a good many acquaintances – of some of whom I should be glad to be rid – and a vast multitude pass before my eyes whom I have not yet learned to like or dislike. Now, sometimes I come gradually to know and value a flower for what it is; sometimes I love one for the sake of its friends; sometimes I fall in love with one all at once for itself, with a love that never leaves me. It was a mingling of the latter two of these loves that arose in me when I saw first the splendid blue pimpernel of this country. I had been intimately acquainted with its red cousin in England; and that feeling blended with the new love for the blue one. It grows to a great size on the sides of the hills facing the sea – that is, the largest are as large as a small primrose. They grow in great multitudes, and are of a deep *burning* blue, as an artist-friend styled it. A slender, snaky, curled grass, that crept along the ground on the tops of the cliffs above the sea, and moved me with some feeling of repugnance, came out in the spring a delicate little blue iris. Indeed, the iris is a common flower here in all colours. A kind of asphodel is common in the fields, and the marigolds and lupins are likewise in great quantities. The varieties of grasses are very strange and beautiful. The cactus flowers had only just begun to appear before we left; but the acacia blossoms were wondrously rich and lovely, and filled the air around our dwelling with their odours. For ten acacia-trees stood on a terrace by our door; and pleasant it was, with the brilliant moon overhead, leaning down towards the earth, to walk on this terrace, looking out over the Mediterranean, and hearing the low talk of the sea and the shore, each a mystery to the other, sounding on far below.

When the warmer weather arrived, I ventured inland as far as the town of Medéah, which lies high among the mountains. Two ladies and myself formed the party; and, seated in the *banquette* of the *diligence*, travelled with much enjoyment, first through the plain of the Metidja to Blidah, and next through the gorge of the Chiffah to Medéah. The day after our arrival in Blidah we strolled out through the town, and soon found ourselves in the market-place. Here one of my companions seated herself on a sack of corn, and commenced sketching some of the Arabs present. We left her surrounded by a group of twenty or thirty Arabs, one of whom, grinning with amusement, was half-leaning, half-lying, over another full sack, and presenting his handsome face for the exercise of her skill. In submitting without repugnance to this operation, these Arabs differed very much from those in Algiers, who would rarely, from religious scruples (representations of the human form being condemned by their prophet), allow their portraits to be taken. Indeed, the same lady had, on once occasion at least, caused the sudden dispersion of a group assembled round a café, by proceeding to sketch it from the opposite side of the street. They hurried on their shoes, rose from their varied postures, and escaped as from an evil eye. Here the men appeared more free, but the women, in one particular at least, less so: for, whereas in Algiers all the Moorish women show both eyes, in the interior the Arab women gather the haik around the whole face except one eye, which you cannot see from the accumulated shade around it. You are hereby delivered, at least, from the sad expression of eyes which, whether from the effect of the setting of white, or from the mystery of concealment, appear invariably beautiful. These eyes are always dark; for, although I have seen blue eyes, on more than one occasion, shining out from these veiled faces, I was assured they must belong to women of Turkish and not Arab descent. How strange some of our fair Saxon women would look in the streets of Algiers! for the French women are generally dark, too. But the dress of the countrywomen is very inferior, of course, to that of those living in the towns. Though when in the street the latter are dressed entirely in white, you can see through their thin upper garments the shining of their gold and blue or red girdles; and the garments are so white that they look ghostly. If you were to see one at the end of a deep narrow passage, emerging from a yet deeper gloom behind, especially if at night and in the moonshine, you would think of a wandering ghost, or the raising of the sheeted dead. But in the country they seem to dress in the same kind of woollen stuff that the men wear. To return, however, to the morning in question. My other companion and I went outside one of the gates of the town, and seated ourselves on the grass. She commenced sketching, and I began to write a note. A little group soon gathered round us, of which two or three were native soldiers in the French army. With one of these, a fine-looking young fellow, who had been in the Crimea, I soon made friends, by asking him to give me a cigarette; the most common way of smoking tobacco here, out of doors, being to twist up a little in paper prepared for the purpose. He granted my petition with the greatest alacrity; and, having prepared the cigarette, proceeded – by inserting a corner of his handkerchief, which had no hem on it, in one of his percussion-caps, and scratching the powder at the bottom with the picker of his musket – to get me a light. He asserted the brotherhood of the English and the Aricans, by laying his two forefingers together, and saying in French that they were all the same. I managed to have a little talk with him in French; after which we exchanged two small coins *in memoriam*, and he presented me with a Turkish one in addition. He then left me, but soon returned, bringing a beautiful bunch of roses, dripping with water, which he gave me. Something within me said, and says yet, we shall meet again.

When we rejoined our companion, whom we left in the market, she told us that after she had finished her sketching, and was going away, one of the Arabs ran after her, and offered her three sous. She asked one who understood French what he meant by it. He said it was to get a cup of coffee with. Their own women have no money, and he had supposed the English women have none either, and wished to show her this hospitality.

The gorge of the Chiffah is threaded by a fine road, one of the many the French have made in Algeria, running along the sides of the mountains, often at a considerable height above the bed of the river. Along the most difficult part of this road, with no parapet on the precipitous descent, and with very abrupt turns, we were driven by a heavy-browed, sullen-faced Moor, the only Moor I remember to have seen driving. To his muscular arm the seven horses he had in hand seemed no more than his four to one of our English coachmen. This part of the journey was very fine; especially one portion, which was crowded on both sides of the ravine with waterfalls of every kind. One of these was very peculiar. It appeared to come right out of the face of the precipice, and after running a little way down, again disappeared, as if it had run back into the rock from which it had sprung. Lovely ferns grew on the sides of the rocks, constantly splashed and dripping with the clear water that ran from above. Though I dislike minute descriptions of scenery, and desire, with Jean Paul, that my friend should have the power of seeing Nature in large masses, yet sometimes the most intense enjoyment flows from no more than a cubic foot of the earth's bulk. I remember one little insignificant hollow, built of rough stones, and roofed over with a stone, inside which tumbled and gurgled and murmured and glided (I wish I might use the preterite *glode*), adown the three feet of its height, a plenteous little cataract of clear, willing water; and all the sides of the tiny cavern were draped and purfled and waved with the maiden-hair fern, with its black stalks and trembling leaflets. But no descriptive arrangement of scenery is of much use. A single unexpected flash of words may now and then throw a real feeling of the scenery on the mind; but the imagination, generally outrunning the intellectual reception of a description, arranges at its will the component elements of the scene, which afterwards refuse to be displaced, even when the mind is better informed. Indeed, a composition painted to express the general feeling produced in the artist's mind by any land-scape, may do more to give a real impression of the nature of a country, in its relation to the higher elements of our being, than the most laborious portrait of real scenes in it, indispensable as these are to a perfect understanding of the whole; because the state of minute observa-tion, the tension of the mind in attending, is inimical to those influences of the whole, which need for their perfection a lake-like calmness and passiveness of the spirit.

It seemed to me noticeable that, both on my companions and myself, the hot south wind from the desert, which prevailed during our short stay at Medéah, produced effects similar to those occasioned by a cold east wind at home.

At length the time came for our return to green grass, and large trees, and grey skies, and the increasing turmoil of confused and confusing progress. On a bright African noon we embarked on board a French steamer for Marseilles. I must mention one man, whose acquaintance I made for the short time it took to cross the Mediterranean and pass the custom-house at Marseilles. We happened to be seated beside each other at the *table d'hôte* of the steamer. I was struck with his Scotch look, and so were others on board. He had nothing of French about him to the eye, only the ear recognised him as a Frenchman. His motions were British, and he even spoke French with more deliberation than his countrymen. But he spoke English well, though he had never been in England, and had only commenced learning it when at the age of forty-five. He was now sixty-three. I asked him if he had read Tennyson. He said he had not, though he had his works on his bookshelves. 'My name,' said he, 'is Tennéson, only spelled with an *e* instead of a *y*. My grandfather used to tell me that we are of Scotch descent, and that our family came over to France with James the Second.' A most benevolent old man he seemed, attentive and kind to everybody. I happened to express a hope that they would not detain us long at the custom-house, else we should lose the train we wished to go by; which was of some consequence to me, as my purse was nearly empty, and I could not get it replenished before reaching Paris. He said, 'I shall be happy to lend you some; make yourself quite easy about that.' And this, though our routes diverged as soon as we reached our port, and I do not know that he even knew my name. He helped us through the custom-house, got a carriage for us, and sent us away with kindness. His benevolence had a happy combination of Scotch solidarity and French politeness.

And now we hastened northward towards our own island; and the skies rose higher, and the stars were paler and further apart, and more of mystery brooded in the wastes of heaven. For we drew nearer to that region of the North where the old hero, weary that the skies rested on the earth, pushed them aloft, that men might have room to live and labour. And so more of mystery in the aspect of the heavenly deeps dwells above the heads of the men who toil and struggle, than over the more noble forms of those who lead an incurious and easy life, waiting only for what will come, and never asking what it may be. And if the more busy and earnest had purer faith in the Father of all, a yet more noble and more dignified repose would pervade the spirit, and, working outwards, impart to the visible form a greater majesty of composure than that produced by the unquestioning fatalism of the Arab.

153

Appendix H

'A JOURNEY REJOURNEYED'

Just as a visit to Algiers prompted 'An Invalid's Winter in Algeria' (1864), so did a summer holiday in Switzerland in 1865 result in 'A Journey Rejourneyed', which appeared in The Argosy, *Dec., 1865–Jan., 1866. On the latter occasion George MacDonald went on his own (*Life, *pp.347–52). This article is here reprinted for the first time.*

My name is Jane. At least that is what I choose to call myself. I want to tell anybody who will listen, what a friend of our family, James Bayley – that is what I choose to call him – told us. I think people will care for it, because it made my sister Lizzie sleep all night with a smile on the face which constant pain makes so white.

There is something very wonderful about James Bayley. Some ancestor of his must have been a magician or necromancer, or something of that sort; for with a few words, flung out anyhow, nothing grand in them, he can make you see such things! Oh! I can never tell them so that you will see them as I saw them; yet I must try. And I know that Lizzie saw them yet more beautiful than I did; for as often as I glanced at her while James was speaking, I saw her face yet more beautiful than the visions his words were raising in my mind. I saw those visions as it were glorified in her countenance. What a pity it is that his words must be withered and shrunk like fallen leaves, by being blown and tossed about in my mind!

But I must explain a little further.

We are a poor family. Even in these days of running to and fro, we cannot manage to leave home, at least not often, and never to a greater distance than Hastings. Brighton none of us like. It seems all made of hard sunlight. But what a shame it is to abuse Brighton, instead of going on to tell you about James Bayley! First, however, I have not quite finished about ourselves. My father was a doctor. I don't think there ever was such a man as my father. Only James Bayley is very like him – in mind and character, I mean. Well, my father died young. So he could not leave much money for us. And yet we were very anxious, both for my mother's sake and for dear Lizzie's, not to leave the old house. So my sister Maria and I go out and give lessons. It is hard work, to be sure; but then think what it is to be able to come home to our house, and our own mother, and our own Lizzie! When I am tramping through the wet in a day like this, with goloshes and an umbrella, thinking of the dreary two hours I shall have to spend with the Miss Drontheims – not dreary because I have to teach, but dreary because I have to teach *them* – I say to myself, 'This is one of my dreams, in which I go tramping and teaching; but I shall wake in my own home with the tea-kettle singing on the hob, and the firelight playing on the curtains of Lizzie's bed. Think of that, Jane,' I say to myself, 'and do your work as well as ever you can, that you may wake with a good conscience.'

I wonder now if this is how people make books, wandering this way and that way, instead of going right on to the thing they want to say. Perhaps, if they went straight, however, they would reach the end before they had made the book, and that wouldn't do. But for me, who am only writing a short – short – essay? paper? article? – article, that's it – indefinite article, that's better – in the hope that some kind editor may think it not quite bad enough for his waste-paper-basket, it is really too bad to go on in this way.

James Bayley is a clerk in a bank. His father and mine were great friends. I am afraid there are not many clerks like James. Do you know he actually *reads* books? Now *I* try to read books; but I know very few people who really do read them. I hardly know whether I do or not. I am sure he does.

James is no richer than we are; and he too has been very little from home. But this summer, an old maiden aunt left him thirty pounds in her will – to go, as she said, into mourning for her. But James said he thought it better to go into gladness for her; and so, when he got his holiday, he went to Switzerland, and thanked God on the top of the Sneezer – I think that is what he called it – that he had come of honest people, and that his aunt had been kind enough to make him a present of the Bernese Alps, which he would keep in memory of her to all eternity. 'Rather better than a suit of black and a mourning ring, isn't it, dear old auntie?' he said.

And the very first night after he came home, as soon as he had had his dinner, he came on to see us. And didn't Lizzie's face brighten up when he came into the room? Indeed, she raised herself higher against her pillows than she had done for the last five years. For mamma, who was in the dining-room, had received him, and said that we were just going to have tea in poor Lizzie's room, and would he mind coming up there, for it would be like a breath of wind to the poor invalid to see such a far-travelled man as James? As if James hadn't been in Lizzie's room a hundred times before! Of course nothing could please him better, and so up he came. And, as I said, she *was* glad to see him, and we had tea by the fire, and, as a special privilege, because he was a stranger, James was permitted to wait upon Lizzie.

When Sarah had taken the tea-things away, and mamma was seated in the easy chair with her knitting, and the fire had been made up, and Lizzie's pillows had been arranged, and her big eyes were looking out upon the circle by the fire – a splendid peach that James had brought her lying on a plate before her – a silence fell over the whole assembly. And the wind, which was an autumn wind, the richest of all the winds, because there are memories in it of the odour-laden winds of the summer nights, and anticipations of the howling blasts of winter, conscious of evil destiny – the wind, I say – the autumn wind – just rose once and shook the windows of the room, as if it would gladly have come in to make one of our number, only it could not, doomed to the darkness without; and so died away with the moan of a hound. And then the fire flashed up as if glorying over the wind that it was of the party; and its light shone in the great old mirror at the back of the room, and in mamma's spectacles, and in Lizzie's eyes, and in a great silver watch-key, an inch and a half square, which James had brought from Thun with him, with a cow and a bell on one side, and a man and a pot on the other.

'Now, James, tell us all about it,' said Lizzie, so cheerily that you would hardly have believed anything was the matter with her.

'All about what, Lizzie?' returned James, with his own smile, which has more behind it than any other smile I know.

'Why, about Switzerland, of course.'

'How am I to do that, Lizzie, when I was there only ten days?'

'You were away three whole weeks.'

'Yes; but it takes time to go, and time to come back. For Switzerland isn't behind Hampstead Heath, exactly. It takes a great deal of travelling to reach it.'

'Then you must tell us all you can, James,' said I.

'Do take me up an Alp,' said Lizzie. 'I am so tired of lying here all day. I climb Alps sometimes at night; but I want to go up one awake, with a hold of you, James.'

'Well, Lizzie, I don't pretend to know anything about Switzerland; but I think I have a little notion of an Alp. I used to think I knew what a mountain was; but I didn't. And now I doubt if I can give you any idea of the creature, for it is one thing to know or feel, and quite another to be able to make your friend know or feel as you do.'

'We will all try hard, James. – Won't we?' I said.

'I have no distrust of my audience,' he returned; 'but my visit to Switzerland convinced me of three things – all negatives. First, of the incapacity of the memory to retain the impressions made upon it. The wonder of the sight seemed to destroy the stuff upon which it was figured, as an overheated brand might burn its own mark out. Second, for I can give you these conclusions as pat and as dull as a sermon – my visit convinced me of the futility of words to describe what I saw; and, third, of the poverty of photography in recording such visions. I did not bring a single photograph home with me. To show one to any of you would be like sending my mother that photograph of golden-haired Jane

(I must write what he said) without one glimmer of the gold, without one flash of the smile – all smoke and shadow – an unvarying petrifaction. I hate the photographs. They convey no idea but of extreme outline. The tints, and the lines, and the mass, and the shadows, and the streams, and the vapours, and the mingling, and the infinitude, and the loftiness, and the glaciers, and the slow-crawling avalanches cannot be represented. Even my mind retains only a general impression. I forgot what had delighted me yesterday.'

'Isn't it like a book, to hear him talk?' said Maria.

To which I answered: 'That depends on what book you mean, Maria.'

I saw I had hurt her, and was sorry directly; but I could not interrupt James to tell her so. I therefore gave her a look that was known between us, and all was right, and I was able to go on enjoying.

'Tell us how you saw the Alps first then, James, and what they looked like,' I said.

'The very moment when I first saw them is burnt out and gone. But the first succession of sights I remember well. I had tried to get a view of them from a great distance across the plain from Schaffhausen, climbing a little hill that lies on the left bank of the river above the falls; –'

'Do tell us about the falls,' said Maria.

'Please don't drag me off the road to places I don't want to go to. That's the way to put all our party out of temper. The falls are beautiful, in spite of the cockney innkeepers and Bengal lights; but I am off for the Alps, and all the cataracts in the world shall not keep me. You will come with me, won't you, Lizzie?'

'Yes, that I will, James,' said the sweet pale-face.

We all begged to be allowed to go too, and promised not to interrupt him again, even to pluck an Alpine rose.

'Come up this steep path then, between a fence and a vineyard. You hear behind you the roar of the falling Rhine; but let it roar. We climb and come into a thicket of small firs, and through that to an open heathy spot, with a plain stretching far away just in front of us. The day is tolerably clear, but it is a chance if we can see the Alps. Sit down on the dry grass. It is dry enough even for Lizzie. A little this way, and you will clear that group of trees. Now think of what you love best, for perhaps you are going to see mountains. Look away to the farthest-opened horizon, through many gradations of faint-shadowy blue. Yes, there are hills, yea, mountains enough – swells, and heaps, and humps, and mounds, and cupolas, all in grey and blue; you can count I don't know how many distances – five perhaps, one rising over the other, scattering forward out of the infinite like the ranks of an ill-disciplined army of giants. But you see no cones or peaks, and no white-crowned elect, and you are disappointed. The fact is, you do not see *The Alps* at all. You see but some of the steps of the vast stair leading up to their solitary thrones, where they sit judging the tribes of men that go creeping about below them after the eating, and the drinking, and the clothing, and never lift up their heads into the solitary air to be alone with Him with whom

157

solitude and union are one. – I forgot myself,' said James, after a pause. 'I beg your pardon.'

'Oh! do talk like that, James,' said Lizzie. 'I can't say I quite understand you, but I feel that I shall understand you when I have had a little time.'

Now, though I am not half so good as Lizzie, I think I could understand James. And if I could not, how could I have remembered what he said so as to tell it as I do now? But then I *think* I know more about James than Lizzie, or Maria, or even mamma does; for I have *poetry* of James's. And when I read it first, I could make nothing of it; and when I read it again, glimmerings came out of it; and when I read it again, there were only some dark spots left here and there in it; and when I read it the fourth time, I understood it perfectly; and when I read it the fifth time, I began to be afraid that I knew nothing at all about it.

'Thank you, Lizzie,' said James. – 'Well, I will let it come when it does come, though I don't *want* to talk in that excited way even about the Alps. It is just like the sixpenny books of the words at the Popular Concerts at St. James's Hall. – Well, you don't see the father and mother Alps; you only see the little ones about their feet; and we must set off at once for Berne – by the railway. And this is rather a trial to us. We don't like to be under obligation to such an obtrusive snake, without a particle of conscience or even reverence in its hydra-head. Its directors are just like the toads and frogs of Egypt that wouldn't even keep out of the king's chamber. Indifferent to its own ugliness, instead of creeping away like an honest snake in quiet places, and coming into notice only when there is no help for it, it insists on sharing the sun with any river; yea, even on crossing the Rhine close above the torture of its terrible fall. It has a right to be somewhere, but not there. If they lay in its way, and it didn't cost too much, it would go right through Strasburg and Cologne Cathedrals; hissing its vile soul out in the chancel, that the passengers might have a peep at the queer fancies of our stupid forefathers, who could care to build such places, and never found out the use of steam and iron rails. Nature, however, will soon cast the folds of her living garment over the unsightliness of its bare mechanism, weaving it kindly up with the many threads flowing from the tireless shuttle of her creation; till at last, it may be, the railroad will cease to offend, except where they have actually stabled its monsters in the very shrines of antiquity. Talk of desecration! A troop of horses pawing the tesselated pavement of a chapter-house, beneath the spreading fountain of its arches of palm-boughs in stone, is a small offence compared to the filthy breath of the engine, as it hisses and screams in the very banqueting-hall of the ancient ruin, which centuries of death could not make a thousandth part so sacred in the eyes of the railway-director as the broad expanse of his own shirt-front, beneath which lies – what? Surely the furniture of his thorax cannot really have sunk through the floor into the story below!'

Now this was a dreadful digression on James's part; and although we laughed at his indignation with the railway-directors, we could not help thinking he might as well have told us about Schaffhausen as run a-tilt against steam-engines. But we dared not make a single remark lest he should stop like an offended llama, and lie down on the wayside beneath the burden of his untold tale.

'On swept the "fire-mouthed dragon, horrible and bright," of which surely Spenser had a vision when he wrote thus; and I blessed the blatant brute in my heart, for it bore me towards those regions of desire which, but for it, I could never have hoped to reach. And suddenly the hills upon the horizon parted as we swept along; and past the gap, in the distance, slowly sailed, like a spectral fleet of ghastly worlds, the hoary backs and heads of the Alpine orearchs. Then in glided the nearer hills, and hid them from my eyes – which straightway scarce believed for very gladness. The moment they vanished, it seemed as if some awful reason concealed them; as if they sat pondering terrible mysteries in their secret place. Again a revealing gap in the nearer mountains; and again the silent terrors flitted slowly by. They were so white, Lizzie! so dreadful! yet so beautiful! Again and again they appeared and vanished, for we seemed to be running alongside of them at a vast distance away. And when the range of heights which concealed them from us drew nearer, and opened at no great distance from our course, then they would rush across the breach in wild haste and white dead-like beauty – great heaps with one or two peaked tops; though mighty with years and growth, yet spectral and savage. They seized upon me utterly. Though not quite like what I had expected, they were much beyond it. Their vastness, more than their hoped-for height, took possession of me. I wonder if mountains strike other people as they do me. I generally see them like strange animals, lying down – almost always couching – with more or less vague remindings of creatures of the known world. Ben Nevis, for instance, seen from the south, always looks to me like a winged elephant; and one of the hills of Morven, away in the west, like a grey-fleeced ram with curled horns, marching eternally forward into space. And now, looking towards the Alps, I saw them like a flock of awful white sheep, lying there under the guardianship of some mighty Titan shepherd – sheep and yet not sheep; warlike and sombrely fierce creatures – perhaps the dogs of the great angels that guard the coasts of our world from the inroads of the fiends. If one of those creatures were but to rise and shake itself! Ah! the stillness of power that lay about their rooted persistency, as they faced the gulf of nothingness, looking abroad, and daring the blank space with existence! For it seems to me, almost always, that the backs of beasts are towards me, and that their terribly quiet faces are looking out into the unknown. – Do you know, Lizzie, I think I understand what gave rise to the grand old fable of the Giants? The Greeks saw human shapes everywhere – as all true poets do. And it is not always the form of an animal that I see shadowed in a mountain, but sometimes the form of a buried man, struggling and straining to rise from beneath the superincumbent mass, which has fallen into some shadowy, almost obliterated correspondence to the huge form which it covers. In one mountain especially, in the west of Scotland, I see the shoulders of a giant heaving away from his neck and down-bent head the weary weight of centuries. I could almost fancy I saw the outline of the knotted muscles approaching the surface in the agonizing effort to rise. But, as I said, I felt, when I saw the Alps, that I had never seen a mountain before, had never known, in fact, what a mountain was. And all the shapes of men and creatures vanished when I came near, and there was nothing there but their own selves, like nothing but·what they are – the children of the great earth, thrust forth from her molten heart of fire into the everlasting cold.

'As I journeyed on I fell fast asleep, for I had slept little since leaving London, and although I heard them around me talking about the Alps, I could not rouse myself to the effort of looking. And so we drew gradually nearer to them. And as my senses returned, I began to regret that I had not conquered sleep and watched the mountains; and I feared that the opportunity was now over. I managed, then, to rouse myself a little and look out of the window. And, between the waves of sleep, I saw a mighty wonder lifted up from the earth, a mountain indeed with snowy head, barred across beneath it with grey dashes of cloud – a child of earth, dwelling in heaven. I was so deeply satisfied that I again fell fast asleep; and that vision shines on with the glory of a dream, for it is "rounded with a sleep."'

'Perhaps it was a sleep,' Lizzie ventured to say, 'and your own soul was making a mountain for itself. I wish I could tell, as you can, the things I see in my sleep. Do you know, I think I have dreams given me at night just because I cannot go out and see things.'

'That I don't doubt, Lizzie. But I am satisfied that vision of mine was not a dream, although it came in the midst of sleep, and its edges were shaded off into it. But as I can give you no idea of the delight it woke in me, the question becomes of no importance.

'I wish, most heartily do I wish, that there were in Switzerland some quiet roadside-inns as in Wales, for instance, where you might be served with *humanity* – with that, over and above corporeal needs, which cannot be paid for, and can only be acknowledged by gratitude. The hotels were the one part of the business which I detested. And then the charges were so high that they left no margin for a poor man like me to be generous. But when I say that I hate the hotels, it is chiefly from a sense of personal discomfort, and not from any dislike to meeting my countrymen, however unlike the mountains they may look. It is a comical reflection, that a large proportion of the English visitors at any great summer haunt, are looking upon each other as intruders – as destructive of the solitude or ruralness of the place; each considering himself only a privileged individual, who may tread the courts of Nature without bringing defilement by his presence, and leaving it behind in his traces. At least many talk like this when they come home. It seems to me the very essence of *snobbery*. No doubt one must meet people everywhere that seem out of their proper place; but for one to glorify himself upon such an election as admits him to a *tête-à-tête* with Nature and excludes others,

seems to me second in enormity only to the same principle of self-
glorification operating in religion. Let him laugh at the cockneys if he
will, only let him be kind-hearted; let him avoid their society if he
pleases, for much of it may not be desirable; but let him acknowledge the
equality of their right in Nature; and when he is thrown into their
company, let him behave, not like the gentleman he considers himself to
be, but like the gentleman he ought to be. Is there not plenty of room
upon those wastes for him and for them? Love will provide a solitude in
the crowd; and dislike will fill the desert itself with unpleasant forms.
Nature cannot be wronged by the presence of any of her children, even if
they have been ill-bred and ill-taught in the fostering city. Greet then thy
brother kindly when he crosses thy path, whether he be fine-toned critic
who gently condescends to the exoterics of Nature, or thy big, bluster-
ing, ignorant brother, who regards all he has seen only as matter of
boastful comparison with what another has or has not seen. Try to
convey the impression of some mighty existence you have beheld; find
that you have made a mistake by the 'Oh! but you should have seen
so-and-so, as I did, on such-and-such an occasion;' and keep not only
your inward temper, but your more inward kindness, and to you the
Alps will be the stair up to the throne of God. But the man who loves not
his brother may crest their highest peaks, may stand on the uttermost
stone, like the living plume of the giant's helmet, and yet never be there.
All that is there will be but the phantom, the simulacrum of himself –
bones, and muscles, and entrails. He himself shall not have ascended the
lowest step leading to the porch of the temple; while the poor cockney
who has no words in which to express himself, save those of the counter
or the Derby, but is free from contempt of his neighbour, may
unconsciously receive some of the essential teaching of these parables in
rocks – these sermons in stone. Who can tell what these visions may
effect in the process of his redemption into the upper air? At least I for
one will hope for him. And I will not believe that these savage solitudes
are less terrible or wild because here and there about their feet, and over
their rocky necks, creep and climb human beings whom other human
beings will not admit as of their kind, because they are not ladies and
gentlemen; these others being in their turn despised by the self-conscious
youth and maiden of ecstatic sensibility, because they can neither
preserve a poetic silence, nor utter new commonplaces about the nature
before them. Would it not be better to rejoice in the knowledge that these
too have escaped for a time from less elevating thoughts, and more
sordid cares; for it is not the interest in to-day's dinner so much as the
anxiety about to-morrow's that oppresses and degrades the man? The
world is made up of all kinds, and why should not all kinds flock to
Switzerland if they please? It will not hurt them, and they cannot hurt it.
If Shakspere had been fastidious as he was refined, where should we,
where would he be now? Despise a man, and you become of the kind
you would make him; love him, and you lift him into yours.'

Now James's talk was more like talk than this; but this is as near as I can give it. And it seems to me worth giving, although another may think differently.

Here, however, he stopped again, and looked vexed with himself that he had been preaching instead of narrating. But presently he recovered his self-possession, and went on.

'It had always been one of the longings of my heart,' he said, 'to be in the midst of the mountains, shut in with protection, and beholding, far above my head, the lonely, sky-invading peaks. Now here I was at last, going up a valley towards the heart of the Bernese giants. It was a narrow valley, whose steep sides were crowded with those up-reaching, slender, graceful pines, the one striking its roots at the level of its neighbour's topmost boughs, to a height casting discredit on the testimony of the poor sense. The valley wound about, like the stream in its bottom; and at one of the turns, it was closed in (to the eye, I mean) by a huge shoulder of rock. And what is that shining thing which lies spread out on the rock, just like the skin of an animal stretched out to dry – grey, and green, and white? There are the four legs and the tail, a grisly sight, notwithstanding the homely suggestion of the drawing-room-rug of people with friends in tiger-breeding India! That is a glacier, no doubt! And a cold breath sweeping down the valley, as if from across its expanse of distance-shrunken miles, confirms my suspicion of the region "where all life dies and death lives."

'Soon I was housed in one of those centres of the "fortuitous concourse" of human atoms, called a hotel; which I hate, I think, nearly as much as any poetic exquisite in existence. But had I not sufficient compensation, when, going down from my bedroom, whose window afforded little view, I peeped from one of those in the public room, and, out in the dimly moonlit night, saw a faintly shimmering ghostly peak far up in the air at distance undefined, haunting the valley, haunting the house – haunting my heart, never henceforth to let it go free from its lovely terrible presence? I had been looking at that same mountain an hour or two before, when the mists on the sides of the valley shone lurid in the sunset. No red touched its cold peaks: it looked on, hard and unresponsive; dead with whiteness, and hard with black rocks. But in the moonlight it glimmered out gentle as the ghost of a maiden.

'It was, however, when I climbed the opposing hill, on the back of an animal called a horse, but made very like a giraffe, that I felt the first full impression of what a mountain is. For across the valley rose a vast upheaved desert, a wilderness of mountain heaps, ranges, slopes, and peaks, of which the nearest outwork, forming the side of the valley up whose corresponding side I was ascending, was a precipice that filled me with horror. This horror was not fear exactly, for I could not fall down *that* precipice whatever other I might fail to escape. But its stony wall, starting from such a height, and sinking plumb-down out of sight in the narrow valley, the bottom of which I could not see, fronted me like the stare of a nameless dismay. I strove against it, and not without success, although the overpowering wonder of that which rose above this wall was not strengthening to the nerves or soothing to the imagination. I knew, even while I gazed upon it, that I should not remember what I saw or felt, or be able to describe it. It was such a chaotic loveliness and awfulness intermingled in savage harmony! – a changeful vision of glaciers, of shifting clouds, of rocks, of falling streams, of snow, of waste wild peaks, of stretches of all kinds of mass, and shape, and surface, mingling in all degrees of height and shadow. And this they said was the *foot* of the Jungfrau! Down below, in the valley we had left, lay fields of bright green, looking as smooth as a shaven lawn, dotted all over with little brown, wooden, toylike houses, the shelter of the goats in winter, to which were visible no paths to destroy the perfect green smoothness. These fields (or indeed *lawns* would be the nearer word) sloped up, with more or less inclination, to the foot of precipices of rock, on the top of which came other green lawns, dotted in like manner with little wooden houses of a rich brown, and sloping also to other precipices rising above them in turn. But the fields grew more rugged and bare upon the ascending terraces, and great lumps of stone came sticking through them, until at last rose the naked mountain, "horrid all with" rock, over which wandered the feeble clouds. And down into the midst of the rocks came the tongues, and jags, and roots of the snow and ice, which higher and higher drew closer and closer together, till the peaks were one smooth, sunshiny whiteness, except where precipices, on which no snow could lie, rose black in the midst, seeming to retire, like dark hollows, from the self-assertion of the infinite glitter, while the projecting rocks looked like holes in the snow. And here and there, over the mountain, lay the glaciers, looking lovelily uneven; fretted, purfled, and wrinkled, like a wrought architectural surface; mostly white, but mottled with touches of colour, which seemed to me mostly green, though at times I could not say that it was not blue; in either case a colour most delicate and delectable to behold.

'Here I put up at a little wooden inn, the only inn I remember with some satisfaction. It was so strange! You would have felt just like wooden dolls in a wooden dolls'-house. My bedchamber reminded me of Gulliver's box in which he was carried about by his nurse, Glumdalclitch, in Brobdingnag. It was just a box with a bed in it – nothing but smooth boards to be seen about you. And here, almost six thousand feet above the sea, potatoes were growing under the windows, and grass was everywhere – a sea of green about the village, whose wooden houses were browned and scorched, and had the ends of their logs furrowed into wrinkles – dividing their annual rings, by the rain and the sun. For all about they were protected by far loftier peaks and walls; so that a height which in Wales or in Scotland would have been a bare rock, was here a food-bearing country, trodden by man and beast, and haunted by lovely butterflies. Indeed, the village is nearly as high as the top of half a Snowdon set on a whole one. And across the gulf at your feet stands the White Maiden, now hidden in thousandfold mist, now dawning out of the cloud. How the purposeless mists do go wandering about, now withdrawing a little, now gathering again, creeping in all shapes over the faces of the hills, and then swallowing all up as if there could be nothing there!

'I wandered about here for a day or two, haunting the borders of the terrible gulf in whose unseen depth lay the pleasant fields of the lower valley, down into which, at night, I had met the deer-like goats trooping with their multitudinous patter of feet, branching of horns, and ringing of bells. But out of this lovely depth below would suddenly sweep up a mass of vapour, as if all beneath had been a caldron set upon an awful fire, and not the green pleasant places of the earth. It would drift about in the valley as in a trough, and then all at once steaming up, swathe and obliterate, in a few moments, the whole universe of heights and hollows, snows and precipices – everything but a yard or two of the earth around me. I would know that all that land of enchantment and fear lay there, but could see nothing, although through the mist might come the prolonged roll of the avalanche falling, far off, down the slopes and steeps of the Jungfrau. This might happen twenty times in a day. Then the mist would suddenly part a little, high towards the heavens perhaps, and you would see a solitary glitter, whiter than the mist – the peak of a dweller in the sky. And the mist would range, and change, and darken, and clear, a perfect embodiment of lovely lawlessness, revealing such dazzling wastes of whiteness, here more dazzling, and there melting into the cloud, so that you could not part cloud and snow! In another place, where the snow had fallen along the ribs of a precipice in furrows converging from the top, you would seem to look upon the fierce explosion of a snow-mine, radiating from a centre of blinding whiteness. And there again would come a sweep of deadly glacier, spotted with green light through the upright scales of its splintered waves – a frozen storm – mimicking the Alpine ranges, jagged into many peaks like them; but all showing from where you stand only as mottlings and unevenness. And all this would be varied to absolute infinitude of bright and dark, of seen and unseen, by the shifting clouds. Standing watching the heavenly show, and rejoicing in the loftiness of some emergent peak, I would say to myself, "There, that is high! But I wish I could see one up there – as high as that! Then I should be satisfied." And out would come another peak away up there; and yet I would not be satisfied. And a higher still would gleam out, like a cloud grown solid, from the liquidly shifting mass; and strange hints would appear of a yet further and higher amid those blankets of the dark beyond. And yet I cannot say that I have seen a mountain-top high enough to satisfy the longing of my eyes; for I fear they cannot, as the wise man says, be filled with seeing.'

'I wandered along the green fields one morning, opposite the waste mountain, and soon came to a shallow green dell, in the bottom of which ran a brawling little stream. It was like many a dell I had seen in Scotland, with a thicket of small, slender, girl-like trees, where the path crossed it: it was like finding a bit of home in the midst of abroad; like wandering in a strange house, in a dream, you know, Lizzie, and all at once coming upon your own room nestling in the middle of it. And I felt a fanciful pity for the little stream which was hurrying away over its stones so fast, nearer and nearer to some terrible slope and headlong fall into the valley below, ere it reached which it might be "pouldered all as thin as flour," in its downward, stayless rush against the steep opposing air.'

Here followed another pause, and James sat staring into the fire, which had reached the peaceful condition of middle age – all in a glow without flame. Again the wind made a rush at the window and died away. I remember it so well, because I saw James start and listen as if it reminded him of some sound he had heard in the wild Alps. It roused him from his reverie, and set him talking again. Turning to Lizzie, he said:–

'I wish I could make you see one of those wildly-grand visions. But I cannot, and it troubles me that I cannot. – I wish I were rich, Lizzie, to take you all there. If I were, you should be carried in a chair, as many ladies are. It would be jolly!'

'Yes, that it would, thank you, James,' answered Lizzie, with a smile that left her lip quivering. 'But when I die, I shall, if God will let me, take Switzerland on my way; and I daresay I shall see it all the better so.'

None of us answered this. And after a moment's sad pause, James went on.

'I left this village with regret. Our landlord was a decent fellow, and the people there did not bore you to buy. But it would be as unfair to judge the Swiss by those met upon the ordinary tourist-routes as it would be to judge Scotchmen by the wandering specimens who, representing themselves as having failed in the "tuitional line," go about among their countrymen in London, infesting them into the purchase of steel pens, which they don't want, at double their value, protesting all the time against charity and obligation.

'But I don't want to talk now about anything but the mountains, and the impression those creatures made upon me. – It is a pity I am so little of a walker. What wonders I might have seen! But you know ever since that attack last winter, a few miles on tolerably level road is all that I can manage. So when I resolved to cross what they call the Wengern Alp into the next valley, there was no way to manage it except on horseback. The mare on which I made that day's journey – let her name be known – she was called Mattie by my kind, half-witted guide, whom I hope to meet again – would carry me safely from the garret to the cellar of any house in London, where the stair was wide enough. At least I shouldn't much mind trying her – throwing the reins on her neck too. But, indeed, that is the only safe way.

'I started on a fine August morning, and zigzagged for hours up the hill opposite that I had ascended before; at first in short – vandykes, mightn't I say, Jane? – then in longer stretches and gentler slopes of ascent; and then back to the vandykes again; now through pine-woods, now along the edge of steep descents, and now along the green slopes of hill-sides. Climbing at last a green shoulder, much torn with rain-torrents, I suddenly found myself face to face with the mass of the

Jungfrau from the valley to the Silverhorn. I could have fallen on my knees before it. That moment I cannot describe. Great clouds crept like pigmy imitations across the front of the mighty real, which towered one rock from its base of precipices up to its crown of snows. And as the rock towered, so its streams fell – in snow from its snow-crown, in water from the caverns of its outspread glaciers; as if the great bald head sought such hair as it could find to cover its nakedness. And ever and anon you might hear the fall of one of its snow-streams thundering from some jagged solitude, which in the space before you might look but a rent in the mountain, or scar upon its rough face. For the avalanches are just streams of snow, now slipping down an inclined plane, presenting from a distance the strange contrast of a slow-creeping river mantled with the foam of a furious haste – sometimes falling sheer over a precipice, a cataract of snow, not, like a river, to gather its force and flow on, but to rest hurtless and silent as death at its foot. One which had been pointed out to me from the other side of the valley, a thin thread dropping far away in the mystery of mountain-tortuosity, we found lying a triangular mass of whiteness, a huge leap at the foot of the Jungfrau.

'I stood and watched the torrents that rushed ceaseless from the cold mouths of the recumbent glaciers. I saw them dilate and contract by the measure of three as they fell; as if some mighty, not yet dead heart within drove, in pulsing beats, the arterial blood of the mountain from a wide wound in its rugged side.

'Now the clouds would gather and half wrap the great thing in their folds, as for an appointed time the weak and evanescent can always obscure the strong and the lasting; and over their swathing bands would appear the giant head of the all-careless mountain. Now they swallowed her up, and she retired equally careless into the awful unseen. I turned my back upon her and descended towards the valley.

'A steep green slope, which we first scrambled up and then rode along; the first of a shower; big cattle, each with its big bell on a broad belt round its neck, glooming through the rain; faster and faster descent of rain-drops; the water running into my boots; steeper and steeper descents; fog, through which nothing but the nearest objects can be seen; a more level spot of grass, with rocks sticking through it in every direction, and haggard old firtrees standing half dead about a stream running over the rockiest of channels and down the steepest of descents not to be a succession of waterfalls, banked everywhere by this green grass – the whole thing making up one of the two places I saw where I would build a house; – singing women; a glass of brandy at a roadside inn; the Eiger hanging over us through the fog, fearfully high and fearfully overhanging, like nothing I can think of but Mount Sinai in the *Pilgrim's Progress*; a scrambling down rocky stairs; and then, through the mist, that for which I have brought you all this way in the pouring rain – the sharp-edged, all but perpendicular outline of the Wetter-horn, close in front of our faces – nothing but a faint mass and a clear edge – the most frightful appearance by far we have yet seen. I would not for a month's sunshine have lost that sight. If I could draw at all, nothing would be easier than to let you see it, as it rushed from the earth through the mist into the sky. A single line, varying in direction, yet in the effect nearly perpendicular, seen through a grey mist – that is all. And all I can say is, *It was terrible*; and there is little good in saying anything, except your saying is your friend's seeing.'

'I see it,' each of us cried.

'Well,' returned James, 'it was just a thing you might dream. No detail – only an effect. But, alas! next day, when we were all dry, air, and mountain, and I, it was so different. The Wetterhorn – and it just strikes me that it must have been named on such another afternoon as that on which I saw it first – the next day, I say, *The Horn of the Tempest* had retired into the hollow of the air; showed not its profile only, but its whole countenance, and yet stood back, and looked nothing remarkable – far lower, exceedingly less imposing. Without being an illustration, it yet reminded me of those fine lines of Shelley – you must not forgive the cockneyism in the third line, although I don't believe he meant to leave it so; and you may see the line ought to end with a rhyme to *storm*:

The Apennine in the light of day
Is a mighty mountain, dim and grey,
Which between the earth and sky doth lay;
But when night comes, a chaos dread
On the dim starlight then is spread,
And the Apennine walks abroad with the storm.

'And this brings me to a question I have thought a good deal about. I don't think I have yet found more than the half of the answer. "*Why do the mountains look such different heights at different times?*" It is easy to say that the cause lies in different conditions of the atmosphere. Very probably – at least sometimes. But still why, while the angle of elevation remains the same upon the eye, should the mountain look different heights? It leads me up to a wide field which I cannot enter now, for you would be wanting me to go home before I was half across it.'

'Do go on, James,' we all said.

'No,' answered James. 'It would be too metaphysical besides. I only say one thing: I am certain that the aspect in which the mountain looks highest is the truest as to height. Nor can any arrangement of clouds make a mountain look higher than it is, or produce an unreal and exaggerated impression of it. But it is marvellous what a difference a few streaks of cloud laid horizontally across the face of a mountain can do to lift its head up in the brain. And that has nothing to do with the atmosphere between. A judgment of the distance has certainly every-thing to do with the *estimating* of the height of a mountain, and the state of the atmosphere has much to do with forming such a judgment; but I am not speaking about *estimating* at all, but about *feeling*. Here is a little bit bearing on the subject which I wrote in my pocket-book at Thun:–

'"Looking across this strange little town to the opposite hills last

night, I thought them lower than Glencoe, or Ben Nevis, or Snowdon – that is, I almost came to that as a conclusion. Now I see them with clouds across them, and they look twice the height they looked before. Take my Ram from Morven, and set Ben Nevis and the two sides of Glencoe and Ben Cruachan in a range on his back, and you would have something like the height as well as something like the aspect of the range in front of me. But it would not impress you so at once, although one of these tops is twice the height of Ben Nevis, and more. Why do we not see them higher then? Just because the *camera obscura* of our minds cannot get its lens all at once adjusted to the facts. And there is another reason: away to the left, in a land of cloud, invisible to-day, but yesterday nearer to all appearance and clearer than those before me now, lie like the flocks of a giant shepherd-king sitting on the circle of the earth, the white-fleeced mountains, whose very calm looks like a frozen storm, and the highest of which is nearly twice as high as the highest of those in front of me now.'
– You will forgive the repetition. I read this to show you how I thought about the varying impression of height when I was amidst the mountains. – I am satisfied just of that one thing, that, so far from a false impression being possible, no accumulation of atmospheric aids to impression can ever generate a feeling correspondent to the facts. Meantime, I have not yet seen a mountain high enough to content me. I *should* like to see the Himmalayahs. Shall I ever look on one whose top goes far enough up amongst the stars to please even my dream-moods? Would those fearful mountains in the moon satisfy me, I wonder? Somehow or other, shall not even our fancies be filled one day?'

James here making a pause –

'Read us a little more out of that pocket-book, won't you James?' said Maria.

'I think I have given you everything worth giving you about the mountains,' he answered; 'and I won't talk about anything else to-night. Well' – turning over the leaves of his book – 'here is another passage which I don't mind reading if you don't mind listening to it. After mentioning the tiger-skin glacier, as I called it, my note goes on thus: 'Soon we saw another greater glacier. – These were the garments of the Jungfrau, and the lady looks very fierce and lovely; and the wind over her clothes smells of no sweet spices, but of cold, beautiful death. This glacier was precipitous, and seemed to come pouring over the sharp edge next the sky, as like white water, with dim glints of green in it such as cataracts often have, as anything motionless – motionless as the face of a dead man – could look. All its forms are of waves and wildly-driven waters; yet there it rests. It thinks, it dreams of what a rush it would make down the mountain-side, if only the frost would let it go.

" 'And now I have seen the maiden in her night-attire, walking in her sleep. You would not know her from an intensely white cloud – cold white – up there in the sky, over the edge of the near, lofty ridge.

" 'How shall I convey an idea of the *prettiness* of the valley below? It is like playing at the country – like the kingdom of the dolls. It reminds me much of the impression produced by Sir Philip Sidney's descriptions of nature in the *Arcadia*. From the stream which runs along the bottom of the valley rise, with much, though varying steepness, and with all sorts and sizes of gently-rounded irregularity, the greenest expanses of grass that heart can desire, up to the foot of an absolute wall of rock, over which in parts look the snow-peaks from afar; and yet they are so near that they are as part of the furniture of your house. If you saw the grass in a picture, you would object to it as badly painted, because too velvety, too soft, too delicately green. It seems as well-kept and mown as a lawn, and all studded over with neat little brown houses, some for men and women and children, some for cows and calves, some for goats and kids, all built in much the same fashion, all pretty wooden boxes with overhanging eaves. The brown earth shows nowhere. All is grass lawn. Indeed, these lower valleys produced upon me the impression of too much neatness, of obtrusive tidiness – as if the Swiss people were the little children whose fathers and mothers, giants up amongst the rocks, had sent them down to play here, out of the dangers of the mighty games going on up there in the cloudy regions. The whole was so pretty as to produce a sense of pettiness. And down upon this gentle, neat, book-pastoral, stare the fruitless hills – no, nothing in nature *stares* – gaze the fruitless hills; or rather, above it they rise, never looking down; rise like the God of the hopeless, who sees, or could see, but heeds not. They are terrible creatures, these mountains. They never love, never have any children; stand there in the cold, and the wind, and the snow, crawled over by the serpent-glaciers, worn and divided by the keen grinding saw of the long-drawn torrents: they feel nothing, they hope nothing. But glorious are the rivers that come down from their glaciers, sweeping blue and bank-full through the lovely towns of the land; and glorious are the mountain-thoughts – the spiritually-metamorphosed reflection of them-selves – they raise in the minds of men.

'"As I stood this evening and gazed at the glaciers, I thought I saw, through the slow clouds over them, streaks that were not of cloud. And straighway out dawned the mountain. Higher and higher parts appeared, and higher and further off still. Such a mingling of cloud and mountain! 'If I could only see that height cleared!' And it was cleared; and therewith the hint of a further drawfed it. And nothing of all this show was quite after my anticipation of mountains and their peaks, but grander; less showy, and more imaginative. How it all changed and changed! And the highest points never appeared at all. And then when the blue heaven came, it dwarfed them all."'

Here James closed his note-book.
  'Weren't you very sorry to leave the mountains, James?'
  'Not in the least. They are not for every-day wear. I think almost I was relieved when I got upon a good space of level land again. I am not sure

that they weren't too much for me, always so high, and so rugged, and so lonely. It certainly was a pleasure to see the horizon far off again. They didn't leave me room enough, perhaps. But I cannot quite tell. And, besides, I have not left them. I have them in me.'

'That is how you have brought them home to us, James,' said Lizzie, in a tone which he thought sounded weary; though, if it was, it must have been from too much pleasure.

'Well, you had better dream about them now, Lizzie,' he said, 'for it is time I left you in peace.'

And he rose to say good-night.

'But do just tell me one thing: Did you go on a glacier at all?' said Maria.

'Only in the most humble fashion – just trod on the tail of one creature that comes down into the bottom of the valley like a dragon of the cold, daring the summer and the torture of the soft wind. It was strange to walk over the rough snow on its surface, or rather gravelly ice, for it was just like rough salt for fish-curing, and feel the warm wind blowing in your face, as, looking up the steep-sloping ravine, you gazed at the splintered pinnacles of the ice, with the light shining green through them. On the tail you could walk, but along the rugged back up there, there was no passing. It looked just like a multitude of alabaster slabs set up on end.'

'Was the colour of the ice really green or blue?' I asked.

'I will tell you where there was no doubt of the blue,' he answered. 'They have cut out, for the sake of poor things like me, a small winding cave into this glacier, entering on the level of the ground. Maria would shriek with delight at the blue of that ice-cave. What matter that human hands made the cave? No human hands could make, no human fancy invent that blue. The very air that filled the hole was blue. And it grew bluer and darker blue as you went in – such a transparent, liquid, lovely blue! bluer than any sky twice condensed, and yet as clear. It was a delight for an angel, that blue! And there was water running through the roof and along the floor; and the walls were so clean, and smooth, and cold, and wet! How delicious that cold after my hot walk! And when I turned to come out, there stood my companion with the face of 'one that hath been seven days drowned' – the ruddy cheek and lips purple, and the white very ghastly. So likewise I looked to him, he said, for the blue changed our *cheer*. And the sunlight was again welcome as I walked back, sucking a lump of the glacier ice.'

'You have not said one word about either of the young men that went with you, James, till this minute.'

'No. I have expressly avoided it, because, if I had begun, I should have gone on bringing them in; and I didn't want to say a word about anything else till I have got the mountains off my mind. Right good fellows they were, and are, and we got on capitally. But I've told you enough for once, and have tired out poor Lizzie. Good night.'

'Go and open the door for him, Jane,' said Lizzie.

And if I had not written too much already, I should have liked to tell you a dream Lizzie had that night. But I won't. I say good-night myself instead.

If you would like it, I may tell you more about James and Lizzie another time.

Good-night.

INDEX

Titles of books, periodicals, etc., are printed in italics. Definite and indefinite articles that begin titles are transferred to the end, e.g. *Lost Princess, The*, etc. The numbering refers to that of the main parts of the bibliography.

WITHDRAWN
(- / 13 / 2022
SAINT LOUIS UNIVERSITY